SUPERVISION

Psychoanalytic and Jungian Perspectives

Edited by
Petrūska Clarkson

Whurr Publishers Ltd
London

© 1998 Whurr Publishers Ltd
First published 1998 by
Whurr Publishers Ltd
19B Compton Terrace, London N1 2UN, England

British Library Cataloguing in Publication Data
A catalogue record for this book is available from the
British Library.

ISBN 1 897635 94 X

Printed and bound in the UK by Athenaeum Press Ltd,
Gateshead, Tyne & Wear

Contents

Contributors

Ruth Barnett is registered with UKCP and BCP as a psychoanalytic psychotherapist. She is in private practice as a psychotherapist, supervisor and trainer. She is Clinical Director of the Raphael Counselling Service and does initial assessment interviews for several organisations. She has written a school textbook of child development and articles in several psychotherapy and counselling journals and books.

Petrūska Clarkson Fellow of the British Association for Counselling and Fellow of the British Psychological Society, is a consultant chartered clinical, counselling and research psychologist, registered individual and group psychotherapist, accredited supervisor and management consultant with some 25 years' international experience, who has more than 120 publications in these fields.

Herbert Hahn is a South African born consulting chartered clinical occupational psychologists and registered psychoanalytic psychotherapist (UKCP, BCP), who works with individuals, couples, groups and organisations. He is a Professional Member of the British Association of Group Psychotherapists and a member of the British Association for Psychoanalytic and Psychodynamic Supervision. His special interests are training therapy, group supervision, staff group facilitation and Social Dreaming.

David Henderson is a member of the Association of Independent Psychotherapists. He is a member of the Core Group which co-ordinates the AIP training in psychodynamic psychotherapy, and in private practice as an analytical psychotherapist and supervisor.

Hugh Gee MA, DPSA (Oxon), DMH is a Training Analyst of the Society of Analytical Psychology and the British Association of Psychotherapists. He is also an ex-chairman of the Society of Analytical Psychology. He is in private practice, and has written many articles and papers, including

'Supervision - Problems in the Relationship' which was published by the British Association of Psychotherapists, 1993.

Jackie Gerrard had a background in social work before training as a psychoanalytic psychotherapist in 1978. She is a Full Member of the London Centre for Psychotherapy and the Lincoln Clinic and Centre for Psychotherapy. She is in private practice and also supervises at Westminster Pastoral Foundation, and is a training therapist and supervisor for the London Centre of Psychotherapy.

Susan Lendrum is registered with UKRC and is an analytical member of UKCP through the North West Institute of Dynamic Psychotherapy. She has written or edited books on bereavement counselling, counselling training and counselling skills in careers work. She is a senior psychotherapist at Hampden House Psychotherapy Centre in Manchester.

Gertrud Mander PhD, IPC is a counsellor, psychotherapist and supervisor in private practice and has worked as a supervisor, tutor and course organiser (Diploma in Supervision) at the Westminster Pastoral Foundation since 1983. As a BAC (British Association for Counselling) recognised supervisor she has been actively involved in the BAC accreditation of supervisors since 1986 and has published a number of papers on the subject of supervision. She has also translated Georg Groddeck (into English) and John Bowlby (into German).

Lesley Murdin is a psychoanalytic psychotherapist with a private practice in Cambridge. She organises training for the Westminster Pastoral Foundation in psychodynamic counselling and psychotherapy where she teaches and supervises. She is the Chair of the Psychoanalytic Section of the United Kingdom Council for Psychotherapy, a member of the Governing Board and is past Chair of its Ethics Committee.

Gabrielle Syme BSc, PhD is an accredited counsellor and supervisor (BAC), and registered both as an independent counsellor and an analytical psychotherapist with UKRC and UKCP respectively. She works in the independent sector and is currently Chair of BAC. Bereavement has been a particular interest and concern; from this, *Gift of Tears* came to be written.

Preface

The professional disciplines of psychology, counselling, psychotherapy, psychoanalysis, and organisational consultancy in Britain have developed unusually (compared with many other countries) separately from each other. Task and role definitions are continuously debated, defended and developed within each discipline and I have discussed these at length elsewhere (Clarkson, 1994).

The definition of supervision has also been much debated. For our purposes here it will be defined as a *contractually explicit conversation between two or more professionals with the purpose of educating, monitoring, and developing service to patient(s)/client(s)*.

A chartered psychologist (who is registered with the British Psychological Society) would expect to be in supervision only while they are in training. 'The criteria for acceptance [on the Register for Chartered Psychologists] state that the person:

- has successfully completed a first qualification in psychology;
- has undergone a further course or period of supervised training in a specific area of psychology, e.g. clinical, occupational, educational [or counselling] or forensic;
- has been judged fit to practise psychology without supervision.' (BPS, 1995, p. 3)

Interestingly, the BPS Division of Counselling Psychology has recently made continuing supervision after qualification an obligation in their code of conduct.

A counsellor (who is accredited by the British Association for Counselling) would expect to be in supervision for the duration of their professional life. The BAC code further requires that an individual accredited member 'has an agreed formal arrangement for counselling supervision, as understood by BAC, of a minimum of one and a half hours monthly on the applicant's work and a commitment to continue this for the period of the accreditation' (BAC, 1994, p. xvii). It would be unethical for a BAC recognised counsellor to practise without supervision.

A psychotherapist (who is on the United Kingdom Council for Psychotherapy register) is currently (usually) only required to be in supervision during training - that is until they are considered qualified to practise independently. It is however a frequent recommendation (customary among humanistic and integrative psychotherapists, and growing among psychoanalytic psychotherapists) that a practitioner will continue in supervision and definitely seek supervision (sometimes called consultation) in cases of uncertainty in order to obtain challenge, information or support. This is analogous to Freud's (1937) recommendation that the analyst seeks additional psychoanalysis at various periods throughout his professional life - particularly when there is a danger that what we may call proactive countertransference issues (Clarkson, 1995) may impede the work. However, we know from Heimann (1950) and Little (1986) that the effective use of what we may call reactive countertransference can be of vital and sustaining importance in the work.

Some approaches would still perceive ongoing supervision for a qualified professional as somewhat indicative of dependency (or somesuch negative), whereas for others, in particular settings such as family therapy, ongoing supervision (of peers and others) is simply an ordinary part of daily professional practice.

As Mattoon (1995) writes about psychoanalysis: 'The training of prospective supervisors is perhaps the least-developed aspect of supervision. Such training has been given little consideration among Jungian analysts, indeed among mental health professionals in general. Such training presumably would include supervision of the supervisor-in-training' (p. 31). Recent experience still suggests that there remains some considerable ambivalence and difference of opinion between analysts as to the necessity or desirability of continuing supervision once a certified analyst. As Dewald (1997) writes:

> For many years, it was assumed that if one were a skilled analyst one would be able to do skilled supervision. It has become increasingly apparent that this is not the case. Some individuals may be effective as the intuitive and empathic treating analyst but may have difficulty in presenting their constructs and concepts in an articulate and understandable form. (p. 41)

Organisational consultants have traditionally lacked the weight of a professional organisation which the other disciplines discussed here have developed during this century. This has had both positive and negative effects. The emergence of the Institute for Management Consultants and its commitment to high standards and ethical professional conduct may affect the field more as the years pass.

Traditionally, however, many if not all management consultants work with other colleagues, giving, getting and sharing supervision (often called 'shadow consultancy', 'apprenticing', 'mentoring', 'staff team facilitation' or another such term).

Many years' experience of training and consultancy supervision to both novice and expert management consultants leads me to believe that this kind of activity is very highly valued. Although not a necessary part of a professional training in this field, nor required by the code of ethics, organisational consultants quite frequently arrange a contract for their shadow consultancy at the same time as they are contracting for a job or project. It is not at all unusual for the shadow consultant's fee to be factored into the overall fee paid for the work by either the consultant(s) or the client organisation. It is simply often felt to be professionally desirable and an effective way to add value and increase profitable and enjoyable work opportunities.

Perhaps we can all learn from the management consultants in other ways too – for example, complaints are seen as a breakdown in the relationship. The first response in this case is to involve an independent facilitator to help to restore the relationship.

> In the unlikely event of a dispute between client and consultant, the Institute believes that it is best resolved through independent mediators. The objective is to resolve the dispute quickly and effectively, and where possible, maintain or rebuild trust and confidence between client and consultant. (Institute of Management Consultants, 1995, p. 2)

In the last decade there has grown a substantial body of literature and research on supervision which is well reviewed and expanded on elsewhere (Holloway, 1995; Carroll, 1996; Hawkins and Shohet, 1989; Inskipp and Proctor, 1993; Clarkson and Gilbert, 1991). Recently, the most excellent *Handbook of Psychotherapy Supervision* under the editorship of Watkins (1997) has brought together an exemplary volume with a most comprehensive and varied coverage of the field and its related research. Hess (1980), Ekstein and Wallerstein (1972), and Doehrman (1976), well-respected for their contributions to the understanding of psychodynamic supervision, and the recent volume of Jungian Supervision edited by Kugler (1995) are other valuable resources.

In an authoritative review of psychotherapy supervision Rodenhauser (1997) found some of the most pervasive problems were that

> standards for competency to provide psychodynamic psychotherapy supervision have not been developed .... There is no generally accepted theoretical model of supervision .... Many supervisors lack skill diversity and flexibility with a variety of theories and practices of psychotherapy .... Supervision of psychotherapy supervisors is uncommon .... Courses and seminars for psychotherapy supervisors are at a premium. (pp. 539-540)

Much of my own work has focused on researching, identifying and explicating the different kinds of psychotherapeutic and supervisory relationship: the Working Alliance, the Transference/countertransference relationship; the Reparative or Developmentally Needed relationship, the Person-to-Person or Real relationship, and the Transpersonal relationship (Clarkson, 1995, 1996, 1997a, 1997b). At the end of the day, our own experience as well as 'the research suggests that the quality of the supervisory relationship is paramount to successful supervision' (Ellis and Ladany, 1997, p. 495).

The purpose of this volume is to emphasise psychoanalytic, psychodynamic and Jungian approaches to the supervisory relationship by several of the most experienced teachers and supervisors of supervisors using these perspectives in a pluralistic setting. Although the contributors come from a variety of basic disciplines ranging from counselling to clinical psychology, they are specifically professional members of the British Association for Psychoanalytic and Psychodynamic Supervision (BAPPS). Each one speaks with his or her own voice from the heart of their own experience. As such it is one of the first core texts of its kind, useful for trainee and experienced supervisors alike.

I undertook this task in honour of my personal psychoanalysts of which there have been four - including two Jungians - as well as all my other supervisors and consultants (Tavistock, IGA, AJA, SAP, BPsS amongst others) and also all the supervisees from a variety of approaches who have deepened my understanding and appreciation over the past twenty-five years for this delicate work in which we are engaged. I wish to thank the contributors and acknowledge all the people, from spouses to patients to editorial staff and Deirdre Donegan, who have made this possible.

References

British Association for Counselling (1994) *Counselling & Psychotherapy Resources Directory* (7th edn.) (I. Palmer, ed.). Rugby: BAC.

British Psychological Society (1995) *Directory of Chartered Psychologists*. Leicester: BPS.

Carroll, M. (1996) *Counselling Supervision: Theory Skills and Practice*. London, Cassell.

Clarkson, P. (1994) The Nature and Range of Psychotherapy, in P. Clarkson and M. Pokorny (eds) *Handbook of Psychotherapy*, pp. 3–27. London: Routledge.

Clarkson, P. (1995) *The Therapeutic Relationship*. London: Whurr.

Clarkson, P. (1996) Researching the 'therapeutic relationship' in psychoanalysis, counselling psychology and psychotherapy - a qualitative inquiry, *Counselling Psychology Quarterly*, 9 (2): 143–162.

Clarkson, P. (1997a) Integrative Psychotherapy, Integrating Psychotherapies, or Psychotherapy After Schoolism? in C. Feltham (ed.) *Which Psychotherapy?* pp. 33–50. London, Sage.

Clarkson, P. (1997b) Beyond schoolism [summary], *The Psychologist* 9: 5.

Clarkson, P. and Gilbert, M. (1991) Training Counsellor Trainers and Supervisors. In W. Dryden and B. Thorne (eds.) *Training and Supervision for Counselling in Action*. London: Sage.

Dewald, P. A. (1997) The Process of Supervision in Psychoanalysis, in C. E. Watkins, Jr. (ed.) *Handbook of Psychotherapy Supervision*, pp. 31–43. New York: Wiley.

Doehrman, M. J. (1976) Parallel processes in supervision and psychotherapy, *Bulletin of the Meninger Clinic*, **40** (1): 1–104.

Ekstein, R. and Wallerstein, R. S. (1972) *The Teaching and Learning of Psychotherapy* (2nd edn.). Madison, CT: International Universities Press.

Ellis, M. V. and Ladany, N. (1997) Inferences Concerning Supervisees and Clients in Clinical Supervision: An Integrative Review, in C. E. Watkins, Jr. (ed.) *Handbook of Psychotherapy Supervision*, pp. 447–507. New York: Wiley.

Freud, S. (1937) Analysis Terminable and Interminable. In J. Sandler (ed.) *On Freud's 'Analysis Terminable and Interminable'*. New Haven: Yale University Press.

Hawkins, P. and Shohet, R. (1989) *Supervision in the Helping Professions*. Milton Keynes: Open University Press.

Heimann, P. (1950) On counter-transference. *International Journal of Psycho-Analysis*, **31** (1): 81–84.

Hess, A. K. (ed.) (1980) *Psychotherapy Supervision: Theory, Research. and Practice*. New York: Wiley.

Holloway, E. L. (1995) *Clinical Supervision: A Systems Approach*. Thousand Oaks, CA: Sage.

Inskipp, F. and Proctor, B. (1993) *Making the Most of Supervision: Part I*. Twickenham: Cascade Publication.

Institute of Management Consultants Brochure (1995) IMC: London.

Kugler, P. (ed.) (1995) *Jungian Perspectives on Clinical Supervision*, Einsiedeln, Switzerland: Daimon.

Little, M. (1986) *Toward Basic Unity: Transference Neurosis and Transference Psychosis*. London: Free Association.

Mattoon, M. A. (1995) Historical Notes, in P. Kugler (ed.) *Jungian Perspectives on Clinical Supervision*. Einsiedeln, Switzerland: Daimon.

Rodenhauser, P. (1997) Psychotherapy Supervision: Prerequisites and Problems in the Process, in C. E. Watkins, Jr. (ed.) *Handbook of Psychotherapy Supervision*, pp. 527–548. New York: Wiley.

Watkins, C. E. Jr. (ed.) (1997) *Handbook of Psychotherapy Supervision*. New York: Wiley.

Acknowledgements

Chapter 2, 'Developing insight through supervision: relating, then defining' by Hugh Gee, was originally published in the *Journal of Analytical Psychology* 41(4), 1997 and is reprinted with permission.

Chapter 4, 'Dyads and triads: some thoughts on the nature of therapy supervision' by Gertrud Mander, was originally published in the *Journal of the Institute for Psychotherapy and Counselling* 1, 1–10 (1993).

Chapter 6, 'Super vision; seen, sought and re viewed' by Herbert Hahn, is based on a public lecture under the auspices of the Jungian Section of the West Midlands Institute of Psychotherapy on 9 March 1996. A previous version entitled 'Unconscious aspects of the supervisory relationship' appeared in *Psycho-analytic Psychotherapy in South Africa* 4, 32-49.

Chapter 7, 'Supervision in bereavement counselling' by Susan Lendrum and Gabrielle Syme, was originally published as Chapter 15 of *Gift of Tears* (Routledge, London, 1992) and is reprinted with permission.

Chapter 9, 'An intervention priority sequencing model for supervision' by Petrūska Clarkson, is a version of a paper originally published in *European Journal for Counselling, Psychotherapy and Health* 1(1).

Foreword

EDWARD MARTIN

Students of the history of psychoanalysis will have noticed that Freud's attitude to the countertransference remained more or less consistent from 1910 when he wrote, 'We have begun to consider the transference . . . and have nearly come to the point of requiring the physician to recognise *and overcome* the counter-transference in himself'. Until Paula Heimann's paper (1950), little was published which either challenged or developed Freud's thoughts. Since 1950, much has been published – not least because there was a lot of catching up to do.

The development of the theory of supervision has suffered similarly. Again, a seminal paper (Searles, 1955) began to stimulate other thinkers to consider the phenomenology of supervision. However the received wisdom – that supervision should be directed at the professional development of the supervisee and not her/his affective inner worlds – arguably still prevails in psychoanalytic understanding. The link between Heimann's and Searles' work is fairly obvious. Countertransference, well hewn, is one of the most potent tools a therapist has. Searles' work on what has become known as either the 'parallel process' or the 'reflective process' in supervision allows (again, when well hewn) unconscious communication between client and therapist to become more clearly understood and the oedipal nature of the supervisory task to be maintained, whilst allowing the supervisor access to the supervisee's affective inner world where this can further the work with the client. Thus the supervisor is able to develop a style of supervision which is therapeutic without becoming therapy.

It is well known that there is a wide spectrum of practice across psychotherapeutic modalities and the place of supervision in these varies. For example, at one end of the spectrum chartered psychologists who are registered with the British Psychological Society would only be expected to be in supervision while training; at the other end, accredited counsellors registered with the British Association for

Counselling (BAC) would be expected to be in supervision (for a prescribed number of hours each month) for the entirety of their professional life. Between these are a number of other variants, supervision being 'encouraged' by some, being 'encouraged if difficulties arise' by others. The critics of the 'supervision for ever' approach emphasise its tendency to infantilise the therapist. Be that as it may, for many if not most therapists regular supervision (case discussion), in one form or another, has become a routine part of their professional lives (Clarkson, 1997).

It is, of course, necessary to bear in mind that 'supervision' is used in a professionally defined manner, namely a 'contractually explicit conversation between two or more professionals with the purpose of educating, monitoring and developing service to patients/clients'. The problems where the roles of supervisor and line manager are held by one person, and the organisational and ethical difficulties these raise, have been widely discussed; the BAC code of ethics makes specific references to these issues. It is also worth noting that in the United Kingdom the role and responsibilities of supervisors have not been legally tested.

At least as hotly debated as the place of supervision in a therapist's life is the issue of whether qualification as a therapist entitles the holder to practise as a supervisor without undergoing any additional training. Thus the status of supervisor or training therapist is given to senior practitioners who have, through publication and participation in public events, allowed their (normally) therapeutic work to be critically evaluated. Indeed, one student recalls a senior therapist implying that supervision was enjoyable because it gave some respite from patients – a perk for one's senior status, as it were. However, supervision *always* implies the presence of the third person, and a case has been made that supervision work has a very different perspective requiring a different technique. Not least because, anecdotally, many trained therapists recall supervision which has been experienced as over-intrusive, sadistic or authoritarian, and there is, anecdotally, more reported sexualisation of relationships between supervisors and supervisees than between therapists and patients. Perhaps because, surprisingly, supervisors forget not only that the transference is given, even in so-called adult–adult relationships, but also that supervision is not purely adult–adult (is any relationship?!), in supervision the supervisee regresses.

Thus in the more recent past specific training in supervision has become one of a number of in-service trainings from which therapists may choose post-qualification. The pioneer of these courses was developed for the pastoral ministry, others started for in-house needs. A scheme for the recognition of supervisors initiated by the BAC in 1988 further created demand for training in supervision covering the needs of both humanistic and psychodynamic therapists.

The papers in this volume, however, have a collective history in that they have either been given at conferences for, or are written by members of, the British Association for Psychoanalytic and Psychodynamic Supervision (BAPPS). This is a professional organisation established in 1989, the members of which are qualified analysts, psychotherapists and counsellors (trained to at least diploma level). All have undergone a significant personal training therapy or analysis and undertaken a separate training or a long apprenticeship in supervision because they recognise supervision to be an additional but related skill linked to the therapy profession. Although BAPPS members are primarily trained psychoanalytically, many have other skills to bring to the task of supervision. They work in various settings, in private practice, in the public and in the voluntary sectors, supervising individually or in groups a range of people – from those using counselling skills to fully trained and experienced therapists.

These welcome papers from a wide variety of experienced practitioners therefore add to the relatively small but growing number of publications by those for whom supervision is more than 'a relief from seeing patients'!

References

Clarkson, P. (1997) A multi-disciplinary perspective on supervision and supervision training. Unpublished manuscript, available from the author at PHYSIS, 12 North Common Road, London W5 2QB.

Freud, S. (1910) The Future Prospects of Psycho-Analytic Therapy. *Standard Edition* 11. London: Hogarth Press.

Heimann, P. (1950) On counter-transference. *International Journal of Psycho-Analysis* 31(1), 81-4.

Searles, H.F. (1955) The informational value of the supervisor's emotional experiences. Psychiatry 18, 135-46. (Reprinted in H.F. Searle's *Collected Papers on Schizophrenia and Related Subiects*, London, Karnac, 1986.)

Chapter 1
Training the trainers: is supervision inherent, caught or taught?

RUTH BARNETT

The development of the profession

Most of the psychotherapies practised today are rooted in, or at least have assimilated substantial amounts of basic theory from, the original body of ideas and practices which Freud named psychoanalysis. He and the early group of followers, including such notables as Jung, Adler, Reich, and many others, had neither training nor supervision in the new treatment. Presumably they learnt through sharing in case discussions, especially Freud's famous 'Wednesday meetings'. There was probably a lot of trial and error, the positive outcomes of which have been handed down to us, together with the 'trials' but with rather fewer of the 'errors'. How else could a new treatment begin?

Before organised trainings were developed, the psychoanalysts and psychotherapists who laid the foundations of our current institutions, such as the British Association of Psychotherapists (BAP), the London Centre for Psychotherapy (LCP), The Westminster Pastoral Foundation (WPF), the Society of Analytical Psychotherapy (SAP – Jungian) and the Institute of Psycho-Analysis, had no other way than to learn 'on the job'. Now, a century on from the creation of psychoanalysis, it is no longer acceptable for someone to begin practising psychotherapy on the basis of lots of experience interacting with people in other ways; they are expected to study and experience therapy in an intensive training, although there is as yet no law requiring them to do so. Without exception, the established trainings now all include supervised clinical work but there is very little organised training for the supervisors.

There are currently so many training courses in various orientations, brands and styles of psychotherapy and counselling that several books have been published on helping would-be trainees find their way through this maze. Perhaps there should be an UCCA-style 'clearing system' for students. One of the features of this rather haphazard way that the field of psychotherapy and its trainings have developed is that far too little attention has been paid so far to supervision in its own right. Although it is beginning to appear now, there is a dearth of literature about the theory and practice of supervision compared to the plethora of writings on psychotherapy and counselling. Whereas supervision of clinical work during and beyond training is accepted and valued, supervision of supervision, even for beginning supervisors, is very rare. Predictions are often made of a person's ability to supervise that are based wholly on what is ascertainable of their clinical competence with patients or clients.

For a long time it has puzzled me why training for supervisors has lagged so far behind training for psychotherapists and counsellors. Are we operating in a myth that supervision is just an extension of psychotherapy that anyone with a few years of clinical practice can move on to? Are we ignoring or denying the complexities of the supervision setting that, though with some parallels, is different from the therapy setting and warrants study and training as a separate activity? Is it just taking time for people to realise the need for more organisation and structure within the profession? In many ways psychotherapy is a profession that has developed very rapidly in its first hundred years and could be seen as 'adolescent' from the point of view that it is still some way off becoming a 'mature' profession with registration under a charter. The current 'argy-bargy' going on between the three recently formed registers, the UK Council for Psychotherapy (UKCP), the British Association for Counselling (BAC) and the British Confederation of Psychotherapists (BCP), could be regarded as a sort of adolescent competition for position as 'top dog'.

The structure of the profession

During my first career in secondary school teaching, I discovered a very complex web of status and power struggles. Sadly, it often got in the way of what a basically dedicated and very professional teaching force was trying to do for its clients, the children. Again and again I was up against the very powerful fears aroused in established and successful older teachers by young graduates from teacher training colleges, especially if these 'youngsters' were keen, hardworking and had new ideas. As deputy head in charge of what was nicely called 'staff and student welfare', I had to try and protect these new teachers from the wrath they 'innocently' engendered in their envious colleagues without dampening the beginners' enthusiasm or exposing their elders to shame – not an easy task.

Who, in the structure (or lack of structure) of the psychotherapy profession, is there to perform this function? Would it be helpful to have the equivalent of a 'deputy head i/c staff and pupil welfare' in each separate organisation? I doubt if many people in the profession would see any value in this, and many might feel threatened. For example, it would be likely to exacerbate the unconscious anxieties of older therapists about not having had any specific training in supervision in response to younger trained supervisors coming along, if there were visible support for the newcomers. As it was originally in teaching, there is an underlying fantasy that the 'old hands' must know what is best and the newcomers can't be in a position to judge until they have a few years' experience under their belts; by which time, hopefully (from the point of view of most of the old hands), they will have become thoroughly suffused with the prevailing system and not have any 'new-fangled ideas' that might 'rock the boat'.

This is so much so that, although there are usually procedures for students to appeal against its decisions, the codes of ethics and professional practice of most psychotherapy organisations do not yet have reliably effective provision for dealing with complaints between colleagues within the organisation. The unspoken presumption is that there will only be official complaints from outside the organisation against its members. Just as the lack until recently of words to describe female experience kept it out of general awareness, disputes between colleagues, especially between the dominant established ones and novices, can be kept conveniently invisible by the absence of any structure to deal with them.

Being confronted with newcomers who have had training experiences they did not have stirs up irrational fears in some very seasoned and proven clinicians so that they imagine they are going to be found in some way inadequate and ousted from their power and status by these 'young upstarts'. Sadly, this mechanism often acts, usually in quite subtle ways, as a resistance to progress and is particularly strong in blocking the development of training for the trainers. It also works to maintain hierarchies and power enclaves that resist change. There seems to be a quite prevalent double-pronged and deep-rooted myth that only practitioners with an aristocratic pedigree (who was your analyst and how many times a week for how long?) and a long apprenticeship can be good training therapists and supervisors. The long apprenticeship insures against straying too far from the 'given wisdom'.

In the long run this sort of structure is likely to become unhealthy. Inherent in it are the dangers of 'cloning' and creating 'incestuous groups'. Too much emphasis on rigour and purity can lead to loss of vigour and finally rigor mortis. Perhaps we should apply Winnicott's concept of the 'good-enough mother' or good-enough parent and focus on the 'good-enough therapist'. What does a therapist need to be capable of to be a good-enough trainer? Surely, the adequacy of our basic therapy trainings is questionable if the graduates from them are not capable of going on to become good-enough training therapists and supervisors? Yet few are doing so at the moment. I wonder why.

Training the trainers

A long hard look at training for trainership, and not just for the few but for the many, is long overdue. The attitude to preparation for other kinds of training, such as teaching and parenthood, has changed dramatically. Parenting is now widely recognised as a job that most people are going to do and they need some specific preparation and training, in addition to their general education, to do it well. What preparation and training does an already well-selected and well-trained therapist need to become a training therapist and/or supervisor?

This is where the debate should begin: based on the acceptance that some sort of training for supervision is desirable. Muddling along and hoping that future supervisors develop their innate ability to supervise or that they will 'catch' supervision skills from their own experience of supervision and working with clients or patients is no longer tenable. Nor should we feel any shame about this in comparison with our 'analytical forebears' who managed to develop and hand down to us such pearls of wisdom through training themselves on the job. The cultural climate we live in now is in many ways a very different one from that of Freud's late nineteenth-century Vienna, and even from the culture our teachers and teachers' teachers trained themselves in during the first two-thirds of the twentieth century.

Two particular changes stand out among the many. As psychological treatment has gained acceptance and popularity with the public, more people are asking for it and an increasing proportion of these are wanting to tackle more deep-seated dysfunctions than used to be the case. Also many of our clientele no longer come with a blind trust in the practitioner as the 'expert', and rightly so, as there has been a substantial shift away from psychological treatment being a 'cure' towards seeing it as a joint learning venture. This leads to the second major change: the focus has moved from psychotherapy being an addition to the skills of someone in one of the caring professions to it being a profession in its own right. A great deal of specialised 'knowledge base' has been developed in the last two or three decades that now underpins more finely delineated skills. That this warrants several years' specialised training to practise psychotherapy is no longer in question. But similar thought has not yet been widely given to supervision.

A body of literature on supervision is rapidly developing, including examples of good practice illustrated with clinical material. Already, several writers have outlined some basic theory based on their own and others' supervisory material: see for example Gediman and Wolkenfield (1980) Eskelin de Folch (1983), Hawkins and Shohet (1989), Bramley

(1996). So far we seem to be at a stage regarding supervision that the writers on psychotherapy, including psychoanalysis, had reached by the 1950s and 1960s. As with psychotherapy then, there are now a few pioneering training courses in supervision. They are bravely developing 'on the job'.

The WPF one-year part-time diploma course in supervision was one of the first. It operates as a weekly half-day session for three ten-week terms and gives intensive psychodynamically oriented practical experience supported with theory seminars and written work. More recently the Highgate Counselling Centre has been offering a similar course. The SAP now offers a series of seminars, and BAPPS (the British Association for Psychoanalytic and Psychodynamic Supervision) is setting up the first degree course in supervision. There are several similarly structured courses in the humanistic and integrative psychotherapy fields.

A differently structured type of course has been developed to cater for the needs of therapists who cannot attend a weekly course. These consist of weekend or whole week blocks of concentrated time at a centre, with 'homework' in between the blocks such as the one at PHYSIS.

As yet we have little data on how effective these different models of training are in different settings. Sharpe (1995) gives a detailed description of block training courses in Norway, Zurich and Manchester. The difficulty of supervising the on-going supervisory practice of the course participants is tackled through the supervision in the training blocks being supplemented with peer-group or telephone supervision between the blocks.

Diversity or disunity?

So far, supervision courses have been developed largely, if not totally, independent of each other. This is something of a repeat of what has been experienced throughout the development of psychotherapy training. Already there is wide diversity between the existing supervision courses, and the problems involved, as can be expected in the development of something new, are legion. The diversity should be cherished. But it makes for the sort of difficulties being experienced currently by the BAC, UKCP and BCP in evaluating courses and setting standards. A great deal of vital energy is being dissipated through hostile competition (as compared to fruitful or benign competition) engendered between these three umbrella bodies. Is it going to be possible to avoid a similar situation developing around supervision training?

The answer is likely to be negative while supervision is regarded by most organisations as an extension of clinical work with clients or patients. There is also the possibility, even likelihood, that each organisation will develop its own supervision training, whether it be in an apprenticeship model or along the lines of a structured course. There is merit in this kind of organisational autonomy in training, but it tends to exacerbate the destructive kind of competition and acts as a resistance to the development of healthy accreditation and clear, fair, and universally workable standards. We have learnt this with psychotherapy trainings; can we avoid the same problem in the development of supervision training?

There may be a chance of arriving at standards of supervision and acceptable means of evaluation and accreditation of courses without the devastating splitting that has resulted in a feud between the BCP and the UKCP. There is a new organisation, the British Association of Pyschoanalytic and Psychodynamic Supervision (BAPPS), which could develop an accrediting function among its already declared aims and objects. Eligibility for membership is currently through the WPF diploma in supervision or any other course of equal standard or equivalent standard of practice through long experience. Whereas it is not possible to avoid stirring up feelings of anxiety and threat in some experienced practitioners, who have not had formal training, when you begin to set up standardisation and accreditation of standards, it should be possible to do so in such a way that the anxiety does not reach a temperature at which it precipitates splitting.

This may depend on how much thought and debate can be managed in an atmosphere of relative safety and non-competition both within and between organisations that have developed training for trainers or are considering doing so. Apart from the usefulness or otherwise of different models and structures for training courses, there is the vast area of content. As yet there is little British research available to guide us, either of the kind based on clinical data or using settings designed for research. Searles (1955) and Mattinson (1975) presented clinical findings to develop supervision theory. More recent writers, Clarkson and Aviram (1997), Gee (see Chapter 2) and Jacobs (1996) have reported the findings of their research. Gee made an interesting analysis of taped recordings of his own sessions with supervisees, and Jacobs describes the process of recording and transcribing one session with his own patient and having it 'supervised by correspondence' with six supervisors, each of a different orientation. These pieces of research are quite fascinating and illuminating. We need many more supervisors to provide 'raw material' on which discussion and debate can be brought to bear.

An issue to be addressed is the advantages and disadvantages of an apprenticeship model compared with learning through sharing in a course group. Here it is interesting to note that the apprenticeship mode of learning the skills of a trade that was so prevalent in the last century is largely out of fashion today. We could do well to examine why, and look carefully at how apprenticeships were managed and their results.

- How far is apprenticeship appropriate and applicable to learning the skills involved in supervising therapists?
- Does the apprentice get something special he or she can't get any other way, or is there a danger of the 'master craftsman' so firmly imprinting his image on the apprentice that he or she is inhibited from developing to full and unique potential?
- Does learning in a course group give enough attention to the individual?
- Is it more likely to confuse the student?
- Is the body of underpinning theory now too large and diversified to be left to the single teacher with their apprentice?
- Can a series of lecture seminars, such as the SAP and other organisations are already piloting, address this problem?
- Are the 'observed live supervision' exercises of the organised courses so important, or can students learn as well in other ways?

These and many more questions need careful thought.

The academic dimension

Finally there is the issue of academia. University staff in counselling and psychotherapy departments and trainers in psychotherapy organisations are already often wary and suspicious of each other. Can the academics really understand and value the clinical aspects of psychotherapy, let alone of supervision? Can the practitioners really acquire adequate breadth as well as depth of knowledge to equip the next generation adequately for such a rapidly changing field? In the words of the song from *Oklahoma*, 'The cowboy and the farmer should be friends!'. Why not a partnership between the clinical-based counselling and psychotherapy organisations and the theory based university departments? Quite a few such joint courses in psychotherapy leading to MA, MSc or PhD degrees have already been started. Are they delivering the goods, and to whose specifications? There is already a lot of disagreement about this. To end on a positive note, there is room for a lot more development to the benefit of both practitioners and academics and, perhaps most importantly, to the benefit of the consumers of therapy – the public.

References and further reading

Bramley, W. (1996) *The Supervisory Couple in Broad Spectrum Psychotherapy*. New York: Free Association Books.

Clarkson, P. and Aviram, O. (1997) Phenomenological research on Supervision: Supervisors reflect on 'Being a Supervisor', in P. Clarkson (ed.) *Counselling Psychology: Intergrating Theory, Research and Practice*, London: Routledge, pp. 273–299.

Eskelinen de Folch, T. (1983) *Psychoanalytic Training in Europe: 10 Years of Discussion*. Bulletin Monograph of the European Psycho-Analytical Federation.

Gediman, H.K. and Wolkenfield, F. (1980) The parallelism phenomenon in psychoanalysis and supervision. *Psychoanalytic Quarterly* 49, 234–254.

Hawkins, P. and Shohet, R. (1989) *Supervision In the Helping Professions*. Buckingham: Open University Press.

Jacobs, M.(ed.) (1996) *In Search of Supervision*. Buckingham: Open University Press

Langs, R. (1994) *Doing Supervision and Being Supervised*. London: Karnac.

Mattinson, J. (1975) *The Reflection Process in Casework Supervision*. London: Tavistock.

Page, S. and Wosket, V. (1994) *Supervising the Counsellor: a Cyclical Model*. London: Routledge.

Searles, H.F. (1955) The informational value of the supervisor's emotional experiences, in *Collected Papers on Schizophrenia and Related Subjects*, New York: International Universities Press, p.588.

Sharpe, M. (ed.) (1995) *The Third Eye: Supervision of Analytic Groups*. London: Routledge.

Chapter 2
Developing insight through supervision: relating, then defining

HUGH GEE

Because of the importance of the practice of supervision of psychotherapy, a number of articles have been written on the subject. Most of this literature concerns supervision of student psychotherapists who are not training to become analysts. Much less has been written about consultations with qualified psychotherapists, and still less about supervision of analytic trainees and consultations with qualified analysts. Of the many articles that do focus on the process of supervision itself, I have not found anything on how insight is promoted by supervisors. I therefore thought that it would be a valuable area to investigate, as it would apply to a central process in the training of analysts. When I started work on this chapter I felt that helping supervisees to develop insight was probably the most important function of supervising analysts and psychotherapists. Newton states, 'To my mind one of the central qualities required in therapeutic work is insight' (Newton, 1961). (I am here using the concept of insight as including the emotional as well as intellectual dimensions of gaining consciousness of what has previously been unconscious.) Interestingly, as Etchegoyen (1991) points out, "Insight" is not, in fact, a Freudian term. It comes from the English language, not only as a word but also as a concept, since English-speaking analysts in Europe and America coined it.' Although Jung uses the word throughout his work, as far as I know he does not make any particular reference to the word as a concept. Nevertheless, the whole of the analytic world seems to be in agreement that insight relates to gaining consciousness of what has previously been unconscious.

How these insights are gained is clearly important in supervision as well as psychotherapy. To study this problem more systematically, I started a research project with the idea of discovering how insights are promoted or demoted in analytic supervision. As my research progressed, I became increasingly aware that changes in the process of the relationship between my supervisee and me were what led to insights, and that my attitudes as supervisor were playing an important part in ways that had not previously been documented.

I am, of course, able to call upon my past experiences as an analyst and supervisor, but for the purpose of my research I attempted to increase the degree of objectivity of my observations by using tape recordings. I have found on listening to the tape recordings that my behaviour is not as I imagined it to be. I used audio tape recordings as opposed to video recordings because of the cost and technical complications involved in using a video camera, and because I think that audio recordings are less intrusive. In either case, video or tape recordings provide a perspective on one's behaviour that is not available in any other way. It is not possible to be totally self-aware while taking an active part in a relationship with someone else. The recordings have provided a view of the interaction that was not available at the time and have therefore stimulated valuable hindsights. Further, as we know from our analytic work, hindsights may eventually become insights. On the other hand, there is the danger of looking at past behaviour from too idealised a point of view, which results in what I call the 'blame game'; that is to say, past problems can be used by the ego-ideal portion of the superego as a way of promoting shame and a sense of inadequacy. If, however, we use the view of the past behaviour provided by the tapes more neutrally, as a learning opportunity, then the record can be an unusually objective teacher, one that reflects like a 'mirror' uncritically, without making comment. I shall return to this issue of helpful 'hindsight' shortly when discussing the issue of 'mistakes'.

With the written agreement of 3 supervisees I made tape recordings of 21 individual supervision sessions; that is 7 supervision sessions with each of the 3 supervisees. During the sessions I noted my thoughts and feelings towards myself in my role as supervisor and towards my supervisee in the role of therapist and towards the therapist's patient. I then listened to the tape recordings and made a brief summary of the sessions. In these summaries I again noted my thoughts and feelings about the interviews and paid particular attention to the nature of my interventions and to the effect they seemed to have on my supervisees. Finally, I also timed the duration of my interventions.

At first I was anxious about the possibility of the recordings interfering with the comfort of the supervisee and therefore the supervisory process. However, on asking each of the supervisees for their views on the effects of recording the interviews, they said one by one that they had quickly become used to the recording machine, and one of them, who had wanted to listen to the recordings, said that she had found them very useful. In fact I offered each supervisee the opportunity of hearing the recording of their supervision session, but only one expressed a wish to do so. What quickly became clear was that the supervisees were quite comfortable with the recording machine, and it was I who had the most negative reaction! (I experienced the recordings as being some kind of superego.) Although this did not last very long it was nevertheless the case that at first I would listen to the recordings and notice all the defects in my work. This gave rise to a certain amount of looking for 'mistakes'. However, over the years of working as an analyst I have come to believe that the concept of 'mistakes' can be used in an unpsychological way and it was this awareness that quickly modified my attitude towards the recordings.

I am unhappy about using the word 'mistakes' in the context of therapy or supervision. The prefix *mis-* means wrongly; the word therefore has a judging quality and it is the case that the word is frequently used in a way that implies blame. I am therefore rather careful not to use the word 'mistake' in supervision. There is no doubt that there are no absolutes in the world of psychotherapy: when we look at behaviour we do so with the benefit of hindsight. With the advantage of hindsight we can examine the hypothesis that we might do it differently given similar circumstances and this is the main point of supervision and the learning processes. Learning is not made easy if the atmosphere is one of blame. That is certainly what I experienced as oppressive when I first started listening to the recordings.

Given, then, that the 'blame game' can be contained, there is no doubt in my mind that the system of recording supervision interviews provides an extremely valuable form of supervising the supervisor. I think that this help can be very much enhanced by the supervisor taking issues raised by the recordings to a discussion group of supervisors.

Getting lost in the therapeutic relationship and slowly differentiating out is a painful process, which can cleverly be avoided by emphasising the value of hindsights. In rejecting this avoidance solution I agree with Astor (1991) who approvingly quoted Waddell's description of George Eliot as 'suffering and moving on rather than explaining and looking back'. Astor continues, 'Institutional learning is often of the explaining and looking back kind, clinging to the safe story telling of reconstruction.' However, there is a value in both looking back and moving forward. Indeed, the process of looking back is part of our need to consolidate which then makes the pain of moving forward more bearable. Without such consolidation, the pain might simply result in disintegration. It is certainly the case that giving examples of reconstructive interpretation is not only negative: it communicates a rudimentary analytic attitude which may be taken into the personality of the supervisee and transformed, through 'suffering', into their individual style.

With all the main Jungian training organisations, supervision (sometimes called training or control analysis) is a requirement and therefore the supervisor's report plays a major part in the organisation's decision as to whether or not the analytic trainee is accepted as a member analyst. It is clear that the supervisor carries great power, and it is likely that candidates for membership in my analytic society and association would find it difficult to make open and honest critical comments about my supervision. I therefore decided not to include in my research supervisees who were in analytical training, with one exception. With this exception there are three important factors:

- I was (and am) in no way involved with this person's training body and the supervisee knew this
- the supervision with this supervisee was coming to an end
- I had already told the trainee that I was submitting a positive report on his work.

It was clear to the supervisee that what he said during the tape recorded sessions would have no effect, either way, on his passing his course of training, or on his future reputation as an analyst. The other two supervisees were already qualified psychotherapists who were interested in having analytically orientated supervision for their further professional development. (In America many would describe this kind of supervision as 'consultation' in that I was not directly responsible for their patients nor were they bound to accept my comments about the management of their work. This distinction could be of value in Britain.)

Given that analytic supervisors are seen by most supervisees as having great authority, it is likely that the supervisor will receive the projection of the parental imago, if not an actual parental transference. Since this is always a possibility in supervision, its effects are a legitimate part of my study. Although this form of research might not be thought of as scientific by some experimental psychologists, as Moustakas (1990) says, 'Heuristics is a way of engaging in scientific search through methods and processes aimed at discovery . . .' Jung (1928a) said something similar at the much earlier date when he stated, 'The sole criterion for the validity of an hypothesis is whether or not it possesses an heuristic, i.e. explanatory, value.' With this in mind I set off on a journey that certainly resulted in valuable discoveries for myself.

The supervisory process

After listening to the recordings on many occasions, I eventually found that my interventions could be placed into five categories:

- interpreting the patient's material
- interpreting the supervisee's countertransference in relation to the patient's transference
- discussing theoretical concepts
- facilitating a supervisory relationship
- facilitating the supervisee's analytic attitude.

Each of these functions would logically play a part in analytic supervision, and it is reasonable to assume that each supervisor is likely to be stronger in one area than another. Before I decided to examine my own behaviour as a supervisor systematically, I would have said that the fifth function – facilitating the supervisee's analytic attitude – was the most important activity, and it was on this area that I expected most of my supervisory efforts to be concentrated. However, on hearing the tape recordings, I found that I was spending most of the time on the first two functions – interpreting the patient's material and defining the supervisee's countertransference. Since I still see the fifth function as being the most important I have, since the self-supervision occasioned by this research, consciously changed the emphasis of my supervisory style. However, I have also learned that supervisees activate certain functions in the supervisor according to their interests, needs and defences, and that I cannot always predict what I will do. Similarly, supervisors will emphasise certain functions according to their interests, needs and defences, and both supervisee and supervisor are obviously affected by the patient's psychology. Thus, which functions are emphasised will depend on the complex communication system that operates between the conscious and unconscious parts of the supervisee, patient and supervisor. With that caveat, I will proceed to report the findings about my own behaviour as supervisor, organised under the five basic headings.

Interpreting the patient's material

The usual procedure in my supervision interviews is for the supervisee to relate what has taken place with the patient since we last met. I do not require them to make process notes of their work with their patients, but neither do I insist on their reporting without notes at the beginning of the supervisory experience. I leave the style of the clinical reporting to the individual supervisee. After the supervision has become well established I sometimes suggest that the supervisee just report without notes, but even so, if someone prefers using notes I accept this arrangement.

Some supervisees like to make notes during our supervisory sessions. Again, I do not object to this, but I have often found that these notes start to be used by the supervisee as a way of avoiding the discomfort of 'not knowing', an occupational stress which I shall discuss in more detail later. When the supervisee merely describes what the patient has said and how the supervisee has responded, I ask also to be given the thoughts and feelings about what has taken place between themselves and their patient. Although this is not the only way of supervising, I believe that this interactional model is the one most commonly used by supervisors in the field of analytical psychotherapy today.

It should be obvious that when the supervisor interprets the patient's material, it tends to encourage the idea that the supervisor will sooner or later give his views on what 'should' have been said to the patient by way of interpretations. I think that this function was, at one time, considered the most important activity of the supervisor. It was thought that through modelling the supervisee would identify with the supervisor's way of working, as might an apprentice in relation to a master tradesman. Let me give an example of this type of supervision.

The supervisee reported that the patient had been given items of silver by his mother over the years, some of which he likes very much and others that he likes less. The 'best things' he stores away, very rarely seeing them, whereas the items that he likes less, he tends to use every day. The patient saw this behaviour as 'silly', because under this system he is not able to enjoy using the 'best things'. As the supervisee talked to the patient about this problem, they discussed how the patient might get the 'best things' out more often. In reporting this matter, the supervisee said that she was aware that their discussion had been superficial and wondered if it had something to do with the patient's fear of being destructive. Without waiting for my comments, she went on to talk about the next day's session.

After a short while, I went back to the theme of putting away these 'best things' and asked the supervisee what ideas she had about the possible meaning of 'best things'. The supervisee said that since the patient's mother had given him these items, perhaps the patient was fearful of damaging them, and for this reason thought that he should put them 'safely' away. I said that since that idea had come to her as his psychotherapist, it was likely to have a value, but added that it might be helpful to try to relate that idea somehow to her relationship to him. After a moment she said that she could not make that connection. I then said (knowing the patient's history of avoiding his feelings) that perhaps we could consider these 'things' as standing for the therapist's interpretations. In that case perhaps the patient was saying that he could most readily use the interpretations that had little impact on him, whereas the interpretations that represented strong feelings had to be put away. Connecting that with the supervisee's idea of the patient's fear of destructiveness, I went on to suggest that perhaps that relates to the patient's fear that this therapist's powerful interpretations, although valuable, will destroy his existing identity. I reminded the supervisee of the value of considering what the patient says in terms of their relationship, pointing out that she had become semi-aware of the need for this focus when she expressed her feeling that their conversation had become superficial. I then said that, with all this in mind, she might then have made the interpretation to the patient that, 'Perhaps you feel that what I say to you is too frightening

and is therefore best put away?' The supervisee thought that what I said
made sense in relation to what she knew of the patient.

Having had several occasions to listen to and reflect upon this intervention, I think that my interpretation may have had some truth value,
but I am quite sure the supervisory process that I have described here is
not the best way of enabling a supervisee to develop the analytic attitude. I think that it would have been of much greater value simply to
have reinforced this supervisee's impression that her discussion with
the patient was superficial and to convey that her knowing this showed
how she was appropriately involved with the patient. I might perhaps
have added that it is always worth thinking about how the material
relates to the here and now therapist/patient relationship. This less
intrusive intervention would have then reinforced her confidence in her
own relatedness, and the necessary insights could have developed later
in their own time and in their own way on the basis of a secure relationship with her patient. I have come to feel that what is important is
to reinforce the supervisee/patient relationship and to encourage the
supervisee to develop a way of thinking that looks for the meaning and
purpose of the material. Paraphrasing an old saying, 'while my speech
could be seen as silver my silence would have been golden'.

On listening to my tape recordings, I observed that I tend to make
interpretations about the patient's material when the supervisee seems
at a loss and is waiting for me to to rescue them from their state of
confusion. However, what I also noticed is that such interventions on
my part encourage the supervisees to be passive and, I think, undermine
their confidence in themselves. After all, with this style of supervising
the supervisor may be seen as the one with all the insights which, had
the supervisee been better, would have also been evident to the supervisee. This way of working not only encourages the idea that the supervisor knows best, more important, it creates a displaced emphasis on
the supervisor's relationship with the patient rather than keeping the
focus on the relationship between the patient and the supervisee.

As a model of direct analytic interaction I found that I was most likely
to make patient-focused reconstructive interpretations when one of
three types of dynamics was operating. I would most commonly do so
when the supervisee was feeling angry with the patient as part of a countertransference of which the supervisee, and often I, were as yet unconscious. The supervisee would then come to me in a state of feeling lost
and helpless, asking me in effect to rescue them from their state of
confusion about the patient's 'irritating disturbance'. In my heroic position of wanting to 'help' the supervisee, I would then make a clarifying
reconstructive interpretation. For example on one occasion a supervisee
arrived to her supervision session with the following account.

She was feeling a bit fed up with her patient. She went on to describe
how the patient had arrived at a session and having sat in silence for

some time he then reported that he had no feelings and no thoughts at all. The supervisee had then asked the patient a number of questions, 'why do you think you are in this state?', and 'what do you think lies behind this state?'. Clearly it would have been more appropriate had she asked herself these questions before saying anything to the patient. Yet my own intervention was also premature: I suggested that the patient may have been feeling angry at not being given the mothering that he yearns for, the anger serving as a defence against the depression in relation to loss.

Although this type of intervention is intended to help, in effect it encourages the idea that the supervisee is a 'no good' therapist. What is more important, it leaves the dynamics of the patient/therapist relationship in the here and now for the most part unexamined.

My second most common occasion for making interpretations about the patient's material was when I was caught up in over-identifying with the patient's anger towards the therapist, which often would cause me to want to show the supervisee 'how it should be done' and even how 'no good' the work had been. Looking again at the example I have just given, my thoughts about the supervisee's 'mishandling' were in part related to my identifying with the patient's unconscious attack upon the therapist and in part because she did not take up the patient's attack in the transference. Yet I (in my irritation) gave an insight which also left out the transference.

The third main stimulus for making such interpretations was when I was in a state of feeling inferior or depressed, for some reason outside of the supervisory relationship. At such times, I would try to repair my narcissistic damage by displaying my 'superior' degrees of insight. The 'eureka' response to an insight reveals, as Jung observed, that insights can have an inflating effect, and their antidepressant action is effective for the supervisor just as well as the supervisee. There is therefore a danger that the supervisor will become overly keen to give insights as a way of getting 'high' on the insight process, rather than enabling the supervisee to slowly arrive at the insight in an organic way over time. This narcissistic use of 'insight-giving' also links with one of the first observations that I made on hearing one of my tape recorded supervision sessions. It was clear that although I was wanting to reveal a supervisee's unconscious involvement with the patient, the communication of this insight into their interaction was frequently done at the expense of not reinforcing the positive work of the supervisee. In this way I put myself into the centre stage position, demonstrating my value, but reducing the value of the supervisee's hard work in building an analytic relationship. Such behaviour not only leaves the supervisee feeling inferior; it also leaves the work with the patient unsupervised. We had stopped looking at the dynamics of the supervisee/patient relationship while we relished my clever hindsights. In all three situations, I see the excessive offering of interpretations as being an indicator that the supervisor is unconsciously identified with a process in the patient that is needing attention. When understood in this way, the pressure to offer interpretations can alert the supervisor to an unrecognised problem in the patient's transference to the therapist.

Interpreting the supervisee's countertransference

This intervention is still regarded by some as a function that should play only a small part in supervision. It is thought by those who hold this view that this is better left to the supervisee's analyst. I have always thought, however, and my research has confirmed, that interpreting the countertransference can be a valuable part of supervision. Nevertheless, when doing so it is vital to keep the focus of the interpretation on the relationship between the supervisee and the patient, and not on the supervisee's personal psychology. In other words, it is the supervisor's job to emphasise that the supervisee's countertransference is counter to the patient's transference and that the focus needs to remain on the patient's transference. I have not found it difficult to stick to this focus, and when I have done so it tends to have a strong impact on the supervisee in the form of insights which lead to a greater understanding of, and involvement in, their patient's psychology. I therefore find this area very important in supervision.

Here, however, the attention of the supervision must be on the supervisee/patient relationship. Continuing with the last example, it can be seen that I could have shown the supervisee how the patient was involving her in a sado-masochistic relationship, by making provocative remarks which led the supervisee into asking slightly persecuting questions. (I say slightly 'persecuting' because they were almost impossible for the patient to answer, and because the atmosphere that the patient created was very much part of the sado-masochistic way his parents had related to him as a child.) This interpretation, which I eventually came round to making, was something of a relief to the supervisee, who before this had felt trapped in her own angry feelings. Another example that illustrates this dynamic is the following.

While listening to a supervisee's description of his work with his patient, I began to feel swamped by the amount of material that he was giving me. At first this resulted in my 'switching off' as a way of protecting myself against the barrage of material. I then became aware of the problem of the outpour and started to think of the supervisee as not being able to contain himself and not being able to clearly present the material. I did not voice these critical thoughts but continued to feel slightly overwhelmed. Then I became aware that the patient was flooding the supervisee with material, and I realised that the patient was doing this as a way of protecting himself against the feared contents of his unconscious life. At that point I shared with the supervisee my thoughts about what the patient was doing to him which resulted in the supervisee feeling relieved. Simultaneously I also felt relieved and no longer overwhelmed.

In this example, we can see how I became unconsciously identified with the supervisee, and wanting the supervisee to relieve me from the burden of my confusion by providing me with a clearer presentation. Only after bearing the discomfort for a time, and pondering on the matter, was I able to put my hypothesis to the supervisee for his confirmation. A constant monitoring of one's feelings and thoughts about the effects that the supervisee is having on the supervisor is necessary and, when achieved, potentially fruitful. Had I not realised that my feelings and thoughts were about the supervisee/patient relationship, I might have concluded that they had to do with the defects in the supervisee, which in turn might have resulted in my giving a negative report on that individual's work. With this supervisee, my reporting on his work was not relevant because he was not a trainee, but this dynamic might operate with a trainee in one's own analytic training program. It is obviously important to consider very carefully the criticisms that one makes as a supervisor about a supervisee: they may stem from an unconscious identification with the relationship between the therapist and the patient.

There is no doubt the relationship between the supervisor and supervisee often resonates with the dynamics between the supervisee and his or her patient. Some have called this the 'parallel process'. Searles (1962/1965a,b) refers to it as the reflection process, but since the word 'reflection' means to bend back as with a mirror, I prefer to use the word resonance. Part of the definition of the word 'resonance' is 'the complex of bodily responses to an emotional state, or of emotional responses to a situation' (*Chambers Dictionary*). Thus, while I think that a supervisor needs to reflect on his or her thoughts and feelings, I feel he or she needs to do so because those feelings are likely to resonate the processes involved in the supervisee/patient relationship. For me they are less parallel than responsive to that process.

Discussion of theoretical concepts

Many think that intellectual educative endeavours should not be part of individual supervision, preferring to leave this to the supervisee's general reading. I would agree that displays of theoretical understanding are not the most important part of individual supervision, but it does seem to me to be a very valuable exercise to relate the patient's material to the relevant theoretical concepts, especially if this does not interfere with the flow created by the focus on the supervisee's relationship to the patient. I have also found, of course, that both the supervisor and the supervisee can use such discussions to defend against the patient's material, or as part of a counter-resistance. A simple example of this problem comes from my work with the first supervisee I mentioned.

On one occasion the supervisee arrived for supervision saying that he was bored with his patient. He then went on to ask me a number of questions about various training institutions. He was aware that I have a strong interest in training courses and methods, and so I was easily distracted. Our general discussion of training lasted for about six minutes before I became aware that we were avoiding the patient. We then came round to talking about how the patient manages to get us to ignore her in exactly the way that her mother ignored her.

There is a particular tendency for supervisees who are not trainees to want to talk about theoretical issues. I believe that this relates to the fact that, having more clinical experience behind them, they are less concerned with keeping entirely focused on the material from one particular patient and are more interested in applying helpful ideas to the understanding of their other patients. Even here, however, I find it is best to keep these digressions to a minimum, and that it is still important to see how such flights into theory relate to the patient. Theoretical discussions with colleagues look at the past from the comfortable position of the present and tend to view psychological issues as if they were static absolutes. They are often used as a way of avoiding our having to become involved with the difficult dynamics of the here and now exchanges. Here and now exchanges are uncomfortable most of all because we may be exposed to what we do not necessarily understand, and so are likely to challenge our existing formulations and even our existing identity. For the same reason, dynamic interactions are the lifeblood of growth. As Jung (1910/1946) said, 'Theories in psychology are the very devil. It is true that we need certain points of view for their orienting and heuristic value; but they should always be regarded as mere auxiliary concepts that can be laid aside at any time.'

Listening to the tape recordings, I kept track of the total amount of time that was taken up by my interventions, and I found that in a fifty minute interview the average total time of my intervention was seven minutes. One situation where my interventions took up a longer period of time than the average was when I was discussing theoretical concepts. This only happened with one of my supervisees, and that one was inclined to find his patient boring. My supervisee insisted that he found these discussions helpful, but I continue to believe that they were mostly defensive in the way that I have already described.

Facilitating the supervisory relationship

Unlike the relationship that most analysts have with their patients, the supervisor relates to the supervisee as a colleague. As Fordham (1961) says, 'I wish to propose dogmatically that it is the supervisor's role, together with that of the seminar leaders, to treat the candidate actively as a junior colleague, and not as a patient, right from the beginning.' It is the case, however, that the relationship is an asymmetrical one in that the supervisor may have more experience than the supervisee. Also, the supervisor has the advantage, for objectivity, of not being as involved emotionally with the patient as the supervisee. It is important for the supervisor to keep in mind that the task of supervision is different from that of analysing a patient: e.g. clinical analysis is concerned with the forming of a professional relationship in order to facilitate individuation which includes analysing the here and now relationship, whereas the task of the supervisor and supervisee is that they are essentially co-workers trying to facilitate the supervisee's ability to analyse the patient through the analytic relationship. Whilst it may not be desirable to stick rigidly to the task of supervision it is necessary to keep the task constantly in mind.

I agree with those who believe that the supervisor should resist analysing the supervisee's personal psychology, but because the supervisee will be inclined to project a parental imago on to the supervisor, it is clearly important for the supervisor to be vigilant for transference phenomena. Since the trainee will be in analysis concurrently with supervision, there are dangers of carrying over dynamics from the analysis and dilution of the analysis by the supervision. Fordham (1961) wrote,

> There is only one suggestion I would like to make here towards management of these rather complex features of training: candidates need to be seen often enough for their analysts to circumvent too much defensive dilution of the transference, and it seems to me beneficial if they are seen on the same day after supervision has taken place or, at the latest, on the next day.

I think it important that all supervisees, not only analytic trainees, have analysis. If the supervisee has never been in analysis, this presents a particular difficulty. It is possible for the supervisee not to be in analysis currently, but if this is the case, it is important for the supervisor to be very watchful of transference manifestations. While the supervisor/supervisee are involved in a transference analysis it is not possible to supervise the supervisee/patient relationship. Again, when the supervisee is not being supervised, but analysed, the work with the patient is being neglected. I have found it helpful to keep the task of the supervisor clearly in mind because it helps to avoid slipping into either analysing the supervisee or excessively analysing the patient. It is, of course, the responsibility of the supervisor to keep the work task orientated. The task being to try to understand the relationship between the supervisee and the patient in order to develop the supervisee's ability to analyse the patient's psychology.

Facilitating the supervisee's analytic attitude

I believe that this is the most important function of supervision. Freud, as is well known, suggested that his technique in analysing was a very simple one. He advocated 'not directing one's notice to anything in particular and in maintaining the same "evenly-suspended attention" in the face of all that one hears' (Freud, 1912). In many ways this is the appropriate attitude of the supervisor, too, and it is by way of adopting this stance that the supervisor can demonstrate the analytic attitude. I have found it helpful to 'ponder' aloud on the material that the supervisee brings; in this way the supervisor can encourage the supervisee to 'ponder' on the material. By 'ponder', I mean allowing oneself to consider the possible meaning and purpose of the material in a relatively non-directive way, allowing the material to 'sink in' while waiting for a thought/feeling/image/insight to arise out of one. During this pondering I believe that there is a dialogue taking place between the conscious and unconscious parts of the self. I think that it is generally accepted that the supervisor is not aiming at imposing one style of working on to the supervisee; however, the supervisor is trying to help the supervisee to develop an appropriate analytic stance. Under this heading I would place such considerations as the nature of interpretations; helping the supervisee to listen to the patient's material; using oneself as an 'instrument'; living with 'not knowing'; carefully observing the patient's behaviour; and valuing the therapeutic relationship. I shall now examine each of these in a little more depth.

Aspects of the analytic attitude fostered by supervision

Interpretations

There is a tendency for some supervisees to think in terms of giving the 'right' interpretation: this clearly reveals an idealistic notion of what a therapist should be. For example:

A supervisee reported that she had been reading something very interesting which she then went on to describe. She then said that she had found these ideas very helpful for herself, and, because this was a universal problem, she wondered how it applied to the patient.

Beyond the problem of therapists applying theory to patient's material, instead of evolving an understanding from the patient's material, I think that this is related to the supervisee having idealistic notions about what one has to know in order to be a good analyst. Such a self-expectation may well be related to the patient also having an unconscious wish for perfection, which would need to be taken up in the context of the supervisee/patient interaction. It is important for the supervisor to communicate to the supervisee that interpretations are essentially hypotheses which are offered to the patient for their consideration. I have half-jokingly said to supervisees that if I had a motto over my consulting room fireplace it would read, 'Listen not to believe and take for granted, but to weigh and consider'. While confrontations on some issues may occasionally be appropriate, I think we should never force an interpretation by confronting the resistance to it critically, because we can never be certain about its accuracy. Moreover, we can never be sure that the time we choose is the right time for the interpretation. For me, the most reliable measure of how appropriate an interpretation may be is how meaningful it is for the patient. Such a criterion of validation does not require the patient's agreement, but only that we observe the reaction to the interpretation, that is, whether or not it has had an impact on the patient. It might be that an interpretation is experienced as meaningless at one time and yet found to be effective at another. Our making of interpretations can be likened to the sowing of seeds, which are scattered rather than dug in, and I have found it helpful to convey this to my supervisees.

Listening

It will seem obvious to say that it is important to listen to the patient, but there is a great deal involved in the art of listening which is by no means easy. Of course we hope to listen with a minimum amount of prejudice and, indeed, unless there is a high degree of acceptance, we will hear very little. In line with Freud's 'evenly-suspended attention' it could be argued that our minds should be cleared of all aims. However, both Freud and Jung believed that the material produced by the patient would mostly have 'meaning' and/or 'purpose'. I have found that one value of this expectation is that it reduces the tendency to judge the patient. Nevertheless, the art of listening to the patient takes some time to learn and can only be mastered when the analyst has established a fairly comfortable personal/professional identity. Without that base of stability, therapists are never free from preoccupations with themselves, and therefore find it harder to listen. Accordingly, I do what I can as a supervisor to support the self-acceptance and identity the supervisee needs to listen effectively.

Using oneself

An attitude that is very much linked to listening is the willingness to use oneself as an 'instrument'. As I said earlier, supervisors often find that their thoughts and feelings will resonate with what is going on in the relationship between the supervisee and the patient. It is also the case that the thoughts and feelings of the supervisee resonate with what is going on inside the patient. Most supervisees, in my experience, find the idea of their being a readable instrument not only valuable but to some extent a relief. A supervisee presented the following.

The patient had described a disagreement with his wife and how, when the wife attacked him, he had not effectively defended himself. The supervisee said that at this point she had begun to feel angry towards the 'unjust attack' by the wife. I suggested to the supervisee that she might be feeling the anger for her patient, who may have felt too frightened to own his anger and had unconsciously activated it in the supervisee who could then become his advocate.

The supervisee in this example felt relieved because she had not known what to do with her angry feelings until this insight differentiated her from her patient. Feelings of relief like these may also be related to the supervisee's discovery that thoughts and feelings about the patient are not just irrelevant or time wasting but are essential to the psychotherapeutic process. At the same time, the therapist learns that it is not necessary to act on such thoughts and feelings but only to reflect on their possible meaning.

Not knowing

Jung said, '. . . we must renounce all preconceived opinions, however knowing they make us feel, and try to discover what things mean for the patient' (Jung, 1934). This attitude of 'not knowing' can also be a relief to some supervisees, because it contrasts with notions they may hold about the need to know 'the answer'. Some supervisees, especially if they are trainees, think that they need to know all that there is to know about analytic theories in order to be a good analyst. Such an ideal is not only a very persecutory one, but also a definite hindrance to their being an effective analytical psychotherapist. It is worth remembering that the origin of the word *therapist* is from the word *therapeutes* which means attendant, which in turn comes from the word *attendere* meaning to stretch the mind towards, as in paying attention to (Partridge, 1958). In order to 'pay attention to' it is obvious that one needs to have a clear mind, one that is free of excessive theory. This attitude allows supervisees to see each interview as being unique and encourages them to be open to whatever their patients bring.

Observing

Alongside the careful non-judgemental listening to the patient can be placed 'observing' the patient. On this subject, Gordon (1992) writes:

There is really so much a person brings along that tells and communicates a great deal about themselves. There are their clothes: what do they wear and

how do they wear it? And there is their posture, the way they present themselves, the way they move, the way they come into the room, how and where
they sit or stand or lie down, in other words what relationship they make –
or find themselves in – to the space, the objects in the space and the person
of the therapist in that space.

The phrases that the patient uses, and their facial expressions, all play
an important part in the communication system, and, as with body
language, the therapist may take in and use this information unconsciously, not always aware of what is taking place. The supervisee who
becomes aware of these ways of communicating may then come to see
the possible meaning and purpose of the communications. Like the art
of listening, the skill of observing is slowly developed and needs much
encouragement by the supervisor.

Valuing the therapeutic relationship

Important as all of the preceding areas are in the development of an
analytic attitude, the area that I have come to regard as the most important is the ability to foster the 'therapeutic relationship'. During my
research I became particularly aware of the well known phenomenon of
the supervisor gaining an insight long before the supervisee. If I told the
supervisee about the insight that had come to me, it would often be the
case that the supervisee would soon after report how this insight came
out, surprisingly, in the therapy too. An example of this was reported by
a supervisee.

*The patient had been talking of how he felt bad about enjoying the
carpentry which he does for the local church. The supervisee said to the
patient that it was as if he could not allow himself to enjoy things in
case that caused them to go wrong. The patient answered by saying,
'No, it is that such thoughts are wrong.' They then fell into silence. I
then said, 'thinking about his Oedipal issues perhaps the patient fears
that you will attack him or lose interest in him if he shows you his
strengths'. The supervisee later reported that she thought that was right
because two days later the patient had talked about how he thought
that his father would not approve of his being successful.*

This anticipatory insight is well known among supervisors and is
clearly described by Searles. Although Searles is right, in my view, to
attribute this process to the fact of the supervisor having a greater
distance from the patient's psychology, I cannot agree when he also
implies that this distance is the more desirable state. Searles actually
states,

A gradual process takes place, over the months and years of supervision, of
the student's identifying with the supervisor's own distance from the

patient's psychopathology, a process which enlarges the degree of observing ego which the student can bring to bear in his work with patients. (Searles, 1962/1965b)

It could equally be said that this identification with the supervisor was at the cost of not understanding and valuing the nature of the supervisee's involvement with the patient. I was therefore dissatisfied with this view, because I still wanted to understand the nature and purpose of the supervisee's involvement with the patient in order to explain, and possibly grant more value to, the process. It would be easy to describe this 'involvement' as 'over involvement', but before making such a judgement I felt the need for a greater understanding of the characteristics of both the involvement as part of the relationship, and the distance as part of its differentiation, and this has led me to a new understanding of insight in general, and the process by which it emerges out of supervision in particular.

Insight: relating and defining

Regarding the achievement of insight, from my observations it seems to me that there are two types of insight: 'ego insights' and insights that arise from the self, 'self insights'. These are not watertight distinctions but indicate a tendency in the way insights come into being. By 'ego insights' I am describing the process whereby we make conscious links between aspects of the material that the patient brings, which includes comparisons between their present behaviour and their past experience. With regard to 'self insights', a way of describing this coming to understanding in an inter-subjective field is as a process, which involves the patient and analyst at first losing part of their boundaries so that they are in a state of 'unconscious identity' in certain areas of their psyches. An image of any kind may then occur from which either the analyst or the patient may begin to find a symbolic meaning. Ordinarily, this process then causes the analyst to slowly separate, or differentiate, out of the state of unconscious identity with the patient which may then result in a defining interpretation being offered. This may result in a change in the relationship between the ego and the self within the patient, which will give rise to a new identity and therefore an improved state of individuality. If there is a defence, or some other blockage to the separating process in the patient, it sets up a tension in the analyst. These defensive states in the patient are clearly seen in the 'repetition compulsive' behaviour which resists change and therefore growth. This state of being in a 'vicious circle' is in fact what the patient brings to the analyst. The analyst, because of being unconsciously identified with the patient, has to work on letting the separating process that will lead to an insight take place within him or herself.

Both types of insight can be operationally defined as the end product of the process of separation or differentiation within the individual and between individuals. An analyst's interpretation is based on an insight occurring on the basis of separation within the analyst, but its well-timed delivery results in the separating process occurring between the patient and analyst, which, in turn, results in a differentiation taking place within the patient. The interpretation – being a powerfully separating distinction – also leads to further differentiations taking place within either, or both, the analyst and the patient. Such differentiation results in the transformation of the relationship between the patient and the therapist and to the transformation in the internal relationships between parts of the individual personality. The healthy analytic relationship is constantly changing in a growth producing direction, which is also a reflection of the dynamic state of the individual personality of the patient under optimal therapeutic conditions. In my experience 'self insights' have a greater transforming effect than 'ego insights'. However, as I have already said these are not watertight distinctions: 'ego insights' are frequently influenced by intuitions, and 'self insights' involve the ego in the latter stages of the insight.

It is my belief that the same process takes place in supervision, because the supervisee brings similar tensions, based on the defences and resistances to differentiate, into supervision; so that the supervisor becomes actively involved in working at the separating process. Mutative insights thus occur between supervisor and supervisee in the same way as already described.

Insights gained through these processes include becoming aware of the transference/countertransference involvements. In the same way, it is the state of unconscious identity and the process of differentiation that provides the supervisor with an eventual understanding of what is happening between the supervisee and the patient. I have use Jung's concept of 'unconscious identity' in the description of this process because I think that the supervisor is unconsciously identifying with the conflicts within the supervisee/patient relationship. The reader will note that I prefer 'unconscious identity' to Klein's concept of 'projective-identification'. I make this choice because I believe that the sharing that I am trying to describe includes the characteristics of the archetypal world and therefore involves deeper levels of unconsciousness than are conveyed by the concept of 'projective-identification'. (Fordham once stated that he saw the 'collective unconscious' as being at a deeper level of unconsciousness than 'unconscious identity', and that in turn, 'unconscious identity' is at a deeper level than 'projective-identification'.) It is also the case that Jung's concept of unconscious identity involves mutual unconsciousness and, unlike Klein's concept, it does not place the emphasis on pathology. In relation to the process that I am describing, I cannot follow Klein, who as part of her description of *projective-identification* says, 'the ego takes possession by projection' (Klein, 1952). In the generation of insight out of a state of unconscious identity, it seems to me that it is the self that projects the function of the ego into the object. However, this may be another difference between projective-identification and unconscious identity.

As a result of the separating from the object, the ego of the individual is slowly reintegrated. It was this process of separating and defining and its resultant insights and interpretations that was the original focus of my research. However, as my self-study progressed I became much more interested in the states of unconscious identity that seemed to precede the insights and indeed I found that the ability on the part of the supervisor to enter into a state of unconscious identity with the supervisee, and the supervisee's willingness to let the supervisor do this, was a necessary prerequisite of insight. There is no doubt in my mind that both the supervisor and supervisee find these states of unconscious identity uncomfortable and that what is yearned for, therefore, is the rescuing and relieving experiences of insight. However, I am now convinced that the states of unconscious identity are almost unavoidable: they are very much part of the early stages of relationship without which the differentiations can neither occur nor be contained. Thus the dynamic opposites of primitive relationship on the one hand and separation, or defining, on the other, are the main ingredients of the growth processes set in motion by analytic psychotherapy and whose tension therefore enters and affects the supervisory relationship.

Unconscious identity

In looking at the origins of this profound level of relationship, it is interesting to read Jung's views on participation mystique, which he also refers to as unconscious identity.

> The further we go back into history, the more we see personality disappearing beneath the wrappings of collectivity. And if we go right back to primitive psychology, we find absolutely no trace of the concept of an individual. Instead of individuality we find only collective relationship or what Lévy-Bruhl calls participation mystique. The collective attitude hinders the recognition and evaluation of a psychology different from the subject's, because the mind that is collectively oriented is quite incapable of thinking and feeling in any other way than by projection. (Jung, 1921)

Although Jung is speaking here to the original nature of relationship and emphasising the loss of individuality, he is certainly aware of the important part this kind of primitive identity plays in early development. For instance, he says,

> In his early years the child lives in a state of participation mystique with his parents. Time and again it can be seen how he reacts immediately to any important developments in the parental psyche. Needless to say both the parents and the child are unconscious of what is going on. The infectious nature of the parents' complexes can be seen from the effect their mannerisms have on their children. . . . This is an expression of primitive identity, from which the individual consciousness frees itself only gradually.

And later when Jung uses the term 'unconscious identity', he says, '. . . the thing of vital importance is that the school should succeed in freeing the young man from unconscious identity with his family, and should make him properly conscious of himself' (Jung, 1928b). Regarding participation mystique, Jung's definition is: 'To put it briefly, it means a state of identity in mutual unconsciousness' (Jung, 1927–31).

In all these examples Jung is keen to show not just the fact of a sharing of an emotional state, but also the importance of the differentiating process. His more positive attitude towards the early stages of relationship can be found in his comments on the 'container' in his clinical amplification of the alchemical vas, and in what he says about Eros, the God of relatedness. In developing the analogy to alchemy, Jung describes how the analyst and patient are like two ingredients in the container of the relationship: as a result of their interaction upon each other changes are brought about in each of them.

I find Jung's conception of the container more appropriate than the way Bion (1963) used the same word, in that his Kleinian formulation has the analyst being the container as opposed to what Jung recognised, that the relationship is the container. It seems to me that seeing the analyst as being the container puts the analyst in an omnipotent position in relation to the patient. I would certainly agree with Bion's observations, however, that the patient may project the holding aspects of the ego into the analyst. I would see this as being done within the containing environment of the relationship. It is further the case that it is the patient who is putting the analyst into that position. But I think it is important that the analyst should not remain identified with the patient's projection. Part of the analyst's task is to help the patient become aware of the shared responsibility of maintaining the analytic relationship which provides the holding for both patient and analyst. For this reason it is essential that the analyst does not identify with the inflated position that he or she is solely responsible for what is taking place. It is, of course, the case that the relationship is asymmetrical but both are dependent on the relationship to contain the interpersonal processes. McCurdy rightly says, 'To experience their patients in "depth", analysts need to allow their unconscious processes to surface and to observe them, in particular their projections, introjections, and identifications' (McCurdy, 1982). I would add that at an unconscious level the patient is involved in a similar process.

Applied to supervision, and the supervisor/supervisee relationship, this means that once the supervisee appreciates the containing aspects of the relationship, it can then be possible to discover in the learning situation that in addition to the destructive dynamics of the unconscious there are also many processes at work that even if equally unconscious, are helpful and positive. The development of the container is one of them, and its acceptance is a sign that the patient knows the unconscious itself can be accepted as a source of meaning and value.

Attachment

The more I have thought about the states of unconscious identity that I witnessed as a supervisor while observing the relationship between my supervisees and their patients, the more I am convinced that it is this process that results in 'attachment behaviour'. My reflections have resulted in my making links with the work of Bowlby and his particularly relevant researches into 'attachment behaviour'.

The importance of Bowlby's work has of course long been recognised. Stevens, for example, said, 'As with most theories espoused by academic psychologists at that time [the 1950s] the primary reward held to be responsible for eliciting infant attachment behaviour was food, and, as a consequence, it came to be known as the "cupboard love" theory. Then in 1958 John Bowlby gave a paper in which he attacked the cupboard love theory and suggested instead that infants become attached to their mothers not so much through learning as by instinct' (Stevens, 1982). In presenting his arguments, Bowlby (1969) made very good use of the work done by Harlow and Harlow (1965). Bowlby was one of the first to recognise how Harlow's experiments with rhesus monkeys showed that attachment was not dependent on the need for food but had its own root. In one experiment, conducted by Harlow, he was able to show that irrespective of which model monkey provided the food, the infants came rapidly to spend most of their time on the cloth model.

Many infant observations confirm that babies enjoy human company and that even in the early days of life babies are quietened by being held and other social interaction. I think that Bowlby's other important contribution was seeing that this behaviour has a survival value which, in terms of natural selection, would indicate as least part of its purpose. Bowlby suggested that the main purpose of attachment behaviour is that it offers us protection from our predators. An isolated animal is much more likely to be attacked and seized by a predator than is an animal that stays within a group. Bowlby also saw that attachment behaviour is always elicited in situations where there is a high degree of alarm. I would add to Bowlby's list of advantages that where people are in a group there are many more pairs of ears and eyes to perceive approaching danger.

From my observation it seems to me that the attachment process involves the parent and child achieving an illusion of oneness (unconscious identity) sufficiently often to provide the child with a sense of security. Narcissistic damage occurs when there is an insufficiency of oneness experiences, which gives rise to overwhelming survival anxieties. The ego developing experiences of separating and defining can only occur, therefore, when there have been enough survival securing experiences of oneness. In other words, the capacity for unconscious identity needs to be established in early infancy otherwise deintegration becomes disintegration.

Resistances to unconscious identity

The supporting of the therapeutic relationship is a very important part of a supervisor's function. In my experience, however, there is a strong tendency among analysts to highly value the separating/defining function which is the emphasis of interpretation, and to experience the primitive relationship processes of unconscious identity as being undesirable states to be dissolved by interpretation as soon as possible. The reasons for this negative attitude toward fusion phenomena are numerous, but I shall describe three of them that I think are expectable resistances to the relationship that is required for healthy supervision.

* First, it is not always realised that these states belong to the early stages of all growth-producing relationships.
* Second, the state of unconscious identity may be very uncomfortable.
* Third, these states tend in our minds to be associated with pathology.

Because these early stages of relationship are likely to involve uncomfortable states of partial unconscious identity, it therefore seems to me vital that the supervisor values and respects this state, understanding that it is one in which the therapist is desirably involved. The contrasting tendency to value the separating processes of interpretation as the royal road to supervision, can leave the supervisee feeling inferior, unclear about what is happening in the relationship to the supervisor, and useless as a therapist.

In one of my earlier examples I showed how both the therapist and I felt flooded by the patient's material, and how I had wanted to rush in and clarify what was going on. In the context of what I am now discussing, it seems to me that it would have been appropriate for me, in addition to showing an understanding of the dynamics of the patient's transference relationship to his therapist, to have first acknowledged the value of the therapist having the feelings of being flooded as part of his involvement with the patient. Since this very involvement demonstrated that he was able to resonate with part of his patient's inner world, I might have chosen to use it to demonstrate his ability to relate to the patient. I see this as an ability because it is sometimes the case that supervisees may defend themselves against the relationship by keeping themselves uninvolved and therefore separate. This is not the kind of separateness that has evolved out of the relationship in the generation of differentiating insight, but the kind that is used against relationship. There is then a very strong tendency for the supervisee to work from the head, to the detriment of the patient.

Defences of the self

The patient will also bring into the therapeutic relationship defences against change and resistance to the relationship. As we know, these resistances are ultimately defences of the self, archaic ways of the patient protecting themselves. In all of the examples that I have given, the patients had very difficult early relationships with one or both of the parents. When resistances in the patient are matched by a similar resistance in the therapist, a vicious circle is introduced.

An analogy that I sometimes use with supervisees is that in order to understand the patient's neurotic 'pits' it is necessary for the therapist to get into the pit with the patient and together find the way out. I will say, 'it is no use thinking that you can remain at the top of the pit shouting instructions down to the patient!' Unfortunately, some potential psychotherapists are not able to become involved in relationships because of a severe degree of damage to their personalities, which is one of the main reasons why I value Jung's original insistence to Freud that people wishing to become analysts must first receive analysis for themselves as an essential part of their training. I am convinced that such psychotherapy for the therapist has done its most important work when the future therapist is undefended enough to accept the states of unconscious identity that are an essential part of the therapeutic relationship. While supervisors may take for granted the importance of the therapeutic relationship, it is when early manifestations of its acceptance are not seen and therefore not validated, that the supervisor can exert a negative effect on the growing professional identity of the supervisee.

Summary

In this chapter I have tried to describe how the supervisor's interventions may be seen as comprising several functions, but that in my view it is the development of an analytic attitude that is the most important of these functions. Insights in psychotherapy are developed out of the therapeutic relationship itself and include ego orientated insights and insights that arise out of the unconscious self. These 'self insights' involve states of unconscious identity between the therapist and their patient which are particularly important for the development of differentiation and insight. Differentiating parts of the personality promotes individuation as described by Jung, but this is not possible without first becoming involved in an intensive relationship. Emphasis has been placed on the importance of the relationship because I think that there is a tendency in supervision to take the relationship for granted and thereby devalue it. In the field of supervision of analytic psychotherapy there is frequently an overvaluing of the giving of insights to supervisees, which may result in their being undermined, and in placing the focus of the supervision on the supervisor/patient relationship. In contrast to this approach, I have found the most appropriate task for the supervisor is to focus on the supervisee/patient relationship. In attempting to answer the important question of how can we supervise the supervisors, I have found it of tremendous help to listen to the tape recordings of my supervision interviews. I have also found it valuable to discuss supervision problems in a small group of supervisors.

References

Astor, J. (1991) Supervision, training, and the institution as an internal pressure. *Journal of Analytical Psychology* 3(2): 180.

Bion, W.R. (1963) *Elements of Psycho-Analysis*. London: Heinemann Medical.

Bowlby, J. (1969) *Attachment and Loss*, Vol. 1. London: Hogarth Press.

Etchegoyen, R.H. (1991) *The Fundamentals of Psychoanalytic Technique*. London: Karnac.

Fordham, M. (1961) Suggestions towards a theory of supervision. *Journal of Analytical Psychology* 6(2): 110.

Freud, S. (1912) Recommendations to physicians practising psycho-analysis. *Standard Edition* 12. London: Hogarth Press.

Gordon, R. (1992) *The Practice of Supervision: Some Contributions*. London: British Association of Psychotherapists.

Harlow, H.F. and Harlow, M.K. (1965) *Behaviour of Non-Human Primates*. London: Academic Press.

Jung, C.G. (1910/1946) Psychic conflicts in a child. *Collected Works* 17. London: Routledge & Kegan Paul.

Jung, C.G. (1921) The type problem in classical and mediaeval thought. *Collected Works* 6. London: Routledge & Kegan Paul.

Jung, C.G. (1927-31) Mind and Earth. *Collected Works* 10. London: Routledge & Kegan Paul.

Jung, C.G. (1928a). The relations between the Ego and the Unconscious. *Collected Works* 7. London: Routledge & Kegan Paul.

Jung, C.G. (1928b) Child development and education. *Collected Works* 17. London: Routledge & Kegan Paul.

Jung, C.G. (1934) The practical use of dream analysis. *Collected Works* 16. London: Routledge & Kegan Paul.

Klein, M. (1952) The emotional life of the infant. In *Developments in Psychoanalysis*. London: Hogarth Press.

McCurdy, A. (1982) In *Jungian Analysis* (ed. Murray Stein). Peru, IL: Open Court Publishing.

Moustakas, C.E. (1990) *Heuristic Research*. London: Sage.

Newton, K. (1961) Personal reflections on training. *Journal of Analytical Psychology* 6(2): 103.

Partridge, E. (1958) *Origins, A Short Etymological Dictionary*. London: Routledge & Kegan Paul.

Searles, H. (1962/1965a) Problems of psycho-analytic supervision. In *Collected Papers on Schizophrenia and Related Subjects*, p. 594. New York: International Universities Press.

Searles, H. (1962/1965b) The informational value of the supervisor's emotional experiences. In *Collected Papers on Schizophrenia and Related Subjects*, p. 588. New York: International Universities Press.

Stevens, A. (1982) *Archetype*. London: Routledge & Kegan Paul.

Chapter 3
Supervision, its vicissitudes and issues of frequency

JACKIE GERRARD

This chapter has arisen out of my own personal experience of supervising for twelve years on once weekly work and for seven years on more frequent work, and was presented at a British Association for Psychoanalytic and Psychodynamic Supervision (BAPPS) conference on this subject.

I feel it is apposite here to quote from a paper by Theodore Jacobs (1993):

> Listening to such self-oriented material you will, no doubt, find your self in the position of the 10-year-old whose assignment it was to read a book about arctic polar bears. When the time came for the boy to give his report in class, he had little to say. 'Did you read the book, John?' his teacher asked.
> 'Yes, ma'am.'
> 'Well, did you like it?'
> 'No, ma'am.'
> 'And why not?'
> 'It told me more about arctic polar bears than I care to know.'
> I'm afraid that in the course of this presentation I will tell you a great deal more about me than you care to know. (p. 7)

I have broken down this vast topic of supervision of once versus more frequent sessions into themes, using the following subheadings:

- My own experiences of supervision
- My own experience of therapy
- Individual versus group supervision – similarities and differences
- Supervision during training versus consultative supervision
- Nature of the patient's psychopathology

- Nature of the supervisee's psychopathology
- Depth of work
- Use of transference/countertransference
- Nature of the supervisory 'facilitating environment'
- Clinical illustrations
- Conclusions – similarities and differences.

For the sake of simplicity I will use throughout the terms 'patient' and 'therapist', which will also cover 'client' and 'counsellor'.

Own experiences of supervision

I have had more or less continuous supervision in varying intensities (from two supervisors per week to one supervisor per month), obviously during training and then since qualifying in 1982. I have been helped by a variety of approaches, initially Jungian, then Kleinian, and in more recent years I have settled down into the (for me) more comfortable and 'facilitating' approach of the Independent School. Where I find I have benefited most is when I am offered a not too critical space to explore, to confess some of the *faux pas* and to discover blind spots, to realise the unthought-through responses I have sometimes made. Good supervision has helped me to discover my mistakes, to see the previously unseen and has offered a space to take my countertransference responses seriously and to differentiate my material from that of my patients. It also helps to express my fantasies and the various distractions that occur in the work with patients.

There was an instance when I felt angry and undermined by a supervisor who, after listening to the three sessions of the week with a patient, made his only comment of the session: 'I can't fault that'. I had not quite realised that I was there to be faulted, or even not faulted – I thought I was there to be helped. It certainly did nothing to decrease my paranoia and feelings of low self worth – always more prevalent during a training course.

I hope that over the years, perhaps almost by a process of osmosis, I have learned from a friendly, affirming, confrontational stance, where I am not too destroyed by realising my errors, or that I could have seen more, that I missed the transference aspects of the communication, that I could have phrased something more appropriately, etc. Here, I would add that it is not just supervisors or colleagues who have taught me this, but also I have felt humbled at times by the sensitivity and astuteness of those I have supervised (and I might say, of the times when I have been 'supervised' by a patient).

A note here on affirmation. Clearly I am stressing how important is the notion of affirmation, and so perhaps I need to offer some thoughts on what I mean by this. I have been helped by a paper from Killingmo

(1995), who distinguishes between interpretation and affirmation, but states they are 'complementary kinds of intervention' (p. 503). He quotes from Sandler and Sandler (1978) 'that in addition to gratifying drive wishes, humans also strive to satisfy wishes for safety, assurance, narcissistic gratification and affirmation' (p. 505). The child needs affirmation of his or her meaningfulness – a feeling of 'I am'. Killingmo says that an affirming intervention is to remove the kind of doubt connected to the experience of reality and a sense of identity, and to convey a sense of *being understood*. Sometimes, perhaps, something as simple as 'yes, I can see why you find this patient so maddening' can be a very affirming experience for a supervisee, convincing him or her that another can understand and feel for the difficulties. I know this experience is no mean thing for me in my own supervision. To give an example: last summer I wrote a paper on love – love of the patient by the therapist. Following the break, my supervisor expressed a real interest in the theme and offered some helpful suggestions. Shortly after this I was supervising a second year trainee at WPF. She had the courage to admit, early on in the academic year, how identified she felt with her client – and then with a burst of bravado said, 'I think I love her'. She was tearful. She felt this was something she should stamp out – that it was a most improper feeling for a trainee in advanced psychodynamic counselling. I think I was able to accept and affirm the reality of the trainee's experience. This first step felt essential, before leading away from that and guiding her towards a fuller understanding of her emotional responses to that client and their meaning in that context.

Now, in the realms of my own supervision, I pause to think of what similarities and differences I find in a once versus more frequent contact between therapist and patient. I feel there are certain nuances concerned with waiting – to what extent does the 'spatula' get offered or be allowed to be found? The luxury of being able to 'wait and see' – meanings, links, interpretations, I find (though some may disagree with me), can be applied to both the work and the supervision when the patient is seen more frequently. I believe most patients being seen on a once weekly basis need 'something' to hold on to and to take away with them, to tide them over the week. There is less opportunity to wait and see in periods of 'nothingness'. In three times weekly work, themes can more easily develop and unfold in all their intricate patterns. Supervisors can encourage supervisees to seek out, hold in mind, make links, even immerse themselves in these themes and developments. In once weekly work, I as supervisee need more help and guidance from my supervisor. In general, the principle of waiting is an important one and applies to whatever frequency of work we are doing. Nevertheless, as I said, I believe patients need something to take away and to hold on to, to bring them back for the next session – just as supervisees need from their supervisor.

My own experience of therapy

I seem to have had a great deal of experience. Before and during my training I saw a female analyst, mostly at a frequency of twice weekly, for six years. I adored her and she was certainly affirming and over time I came to feel loved by her. She will always have my love and gratitude. Some time later, I saw a male analyst for five years three times weekly and although I experienced a certain amount of rage and frustration, there was also regard, respect, acceptance and affirmation. I learned from him that I could be loveable to a man whom I deeply respected, without the erotic and sexual feelings and fantasies having to be enacted. I left feeling more satisfied with myself as a person and as a therapist. I returned to him two years later, during a further training course, for a two year period of once weekly therapy. It may be difficult to judge the efficacy of this frequency in isolation as, to quote my analyst, it was 'on the back' of the five year three times weekly analysis. It certainly had value, but I know that during that latter time my feelings were not of the same depth and strength. I was less infantile, less demanding, more adult, in spite of the fact that I do have a belief, as Gertrud Mander emphasises in her 1995 paper, that many patients are able to regress and progress in once weekly work.

More recently, I began a new analysis at a frequency of four times weekly, again with a female analyst. Within this experience I have discovered not just depths of hatred, rage and disappointment, but my own destructiveness. Without going further into personal detail, I think what I have learned is that it is only more frequent analytic work that can sustain a relationship through such tidal waves of negative transference. Had I been seeing my analyst once weekly during these storms of violent feelings, then I would certainly have aborted the analysis. But then again, I cannot be sure the same feelings would have been aroused in this less frequent contact.

This must have implications for supervision and I think links up with what I have said about the need for something to hold on to in once weekly work. The degree of negative transference that can be aroused, contained and interpreted is, I feel, reflective of the frequency of contact between therapist and patient. Let me here quote from Winnicott (1971):

> Without the experience of maximum destructiveness (object not protected) the subject never places the analyst outside and therefore can never do more than experience a kind of self-analysis, using the analyst as a projection of a part of the self . . . The patient may even enjoy the analytic experience but will not fundamentally change. (p. 107) . . . This quality of 'always being destroyed' makes the reality of the supervising object felt as such, strengthens the feeling tone, and contributes to object-constancy. The object can now be used. (p. 110)

Individual versus group supervision

Since 1984 I have been working with groups of 3–4 trainees working towards their Diploma in Advanced Psychodynamic Counselling. Their work with clients is always once weekly and I find a range of sophistication in technique, capacities for empathy, insight and interpretation. Group supervision is a special beast. There are many pros and cons of supervising and being supervised in this way. Some of the advantages, with which many of you will already be familiar, are:

- other members of the group learning to supervise
- learning about different kinds of patients
- teaching me, by feedback, by seeing what I do not see, by confronting each other.

Some of the disadvantages are:

- insufficient time and space for in-depth exploration of all the client material
- acute rivalry and competitiveness intruding into the task
- fear on the trainees' part of making personal revelations – either in terms of their own psychopathology, or in what was felt, said and done in the sessions.

These once weekly groups, however, which I still run, do challenge me and keep me alert and thinking.

I have also supervised two groups of psychotherapy trainees. These differ from the counsellors' groups in two main respects: the frequency of contact with the patients and the fact that we concentrate on just one patient per trainee. This is certainly a bonus for the supervisor, as far fewer patients have to be held in mind from week to week. Trainee psychotherapists are all working at a greater frequency than once weekly. Patterns of interaction between trainee and patient are seen more easily. Attention to detail means, however, that the trainee therapist can feel exposed quite quickly in this type of group supervision. It can be felt as a persecutory, humiliating experience, as well as possibly an enriching one. Although I know that fear of exposure also obtains in counsellor supervision groups, I feel there is more intense anxiety in psychotherapy group supervision. Hence, perhaps, why in most trainings this has now been stopped and supervision of psychotherapy trainees takes place individually. I realise individual supervision can also be a persecutory experience depending on how the supervisor handles the difficulties, particularly in regard to transferences and resistances in the clinical work and in the supervisory relationship.

Here I am also including the supervisor's transferences to the supervisee, which have to be constantly monitored in individual supervision (the group somehow helps me to monitor these in group supervision).

From my own experience, I know I can feel two extremes – on the one hand protective and defensive of the trainee and his or her work in the light of criticism from the training institution; and, in complete contrast, disparaging of the trainee's work wondering how he or she managed to get selected for a training. Many other transferences also occur. If these, and also the idealisations and denigrations do not get resolved after a while on my part, then I will need supervision of my supervision, or I will need to explore the supervisory relationship in my analysis, in the hope that any distortions, projections or impasses can be resolved. Of course, the 'parallel process', the reflection of the relationship between therapist and patient finding its way into that between supervisor and supervisee, has also to be taken into account.

With regard to this, I was interested to read Stimmel's paper, 'Resistance to awareness of the supervisor's transference, with special reference to the parallel process' (1995). In this, she spells out her thoughts, with clinical illustrations, about the fact that an understanding of the parallel process, invaluable though it is – she calls it 'one of the conceptual bridges between treatment and supervision' (p. 615) – 'may be used also as a resistance to awareness of transference phenomena within the supervisor in relation to the supervisee' (p. 609). So, she concludes, 'the parallel processes were way-stations' . . . but 'it was necessary, however, to continue on to a more complete destination, one which included understanding how the way-station had almost become a detour'. 'It is when the parallel process interferes with knowing herself as well as she could that the supervisor has employed this concept in the service of resistance' (p. 616).

I think there is less danger of this in group supervision – the group serves to reflect more for me and each other what is going on. An incident from last year's supervision group comes to mind. In a new second year supervision group, a male trainee presented a counselling session. His responses to his client were Rogerian, to say the least – he continually repeated the client's words. It was as if he had regressed, or not begun to do psychodynamic work in the first year. I found myself scathing – had he never heard of the transference – what had he been doing all last year? He was naturally devastated and angry with me. The following week we explored in the group what had happened. He admitted how useful it had been. He had taken his fury to therapy, understood it in terms of his reaction to perceived powerful women in his life, and seen how he had set himself up to be knocked down. The other group members 'supervised' me. They felt what I had said to be appropriate, though the way I had said it was very harsh. I had then to explore in my own space what he had aroused in me. The outcome was that the trainee's work changed, and subsequently he demonstrated that he had a grasp of the transference and a capacity to think about and to use it.

Had this happened in individual supervision, I hope we would have been able to find a similar resolution, but it would have been without the help of the feedback from the other group members which provided a holding and a safety net.

Supervision during training versus consultative supervision

Personally, I find that this issue needs careful attention. It does not, perhaps, relate specifically to the number of times per week the patient is being seen, but it is an essential dimension when taking into account the supervisor/supervisee relationship. In most cases where training and assessment are involved and the trainee's future career and qualification are at stake, anxiety and fear of failure must play a very large part. Perhaps we have all been guilty of concealing something we said, that at the time, or in a subsequent process recording, sounded ignorant, crass, not thought through. Then there is the degree of anxiety in holding a training patient. Trainees invariably see a patient's premature leaving or a reduction in sessions, not only as a sense of personal failure but with a sinking heart as they know their training time will be prolonged. This concerns predominantly psychotherapy trainees, but can also be felt as a deep sense of inadequacy by trainee counsellors. The role of the supervisor at this time is to try and help the trainee understand the patient's leaving as clearly as possible and, at the same time, to endeavour to preserve some measure of the trainee's self esteem. Perhaps a broad brush distinction between training supervision and consultative supervision is that in the mind of the supervisee would be: 'What does this supervisor think of me?' in assessment supervision, whereas in consultative supervision might be, 'What does the supervisor think is happening between the patient and myself?' I should note here the dynamics of the power relationship that are highly relevant in training supervision, where generally there is likely to be less confrontation of the supervisor by supervisee.

As supervisor, I personally feel a greater freedom when I am not involved in the training and assessment process. Nevertheless, every coin has two sides. There is something to be said for the challenge of helping a trainee (hopefully) through the provision of a 'facilitating environment' to reach the required standard of work in a given time. It may be, therefore, that for some supervisors the task of supervising during training provides greater challenge and stimulation.

Nature of the patient's psychopathology

In a world where training and assessment are not the fundamental issues, the supervisor and supervisee may begin with the luxury of thinking together about the optimum frequency for a particular patient to be seen in therapy. As well as depending on issues of time and money and experience of the therapist, this will also relate to the nature of the patient's psychopathology. These considerations also link up with the personal training, orientation and biases of the supervisor, but it is important to try to begin work at the appropriate frequency for the patient because for many patients a pattern once established may be difficult to change (involving renegotiation of 'the frame'). In my clinical material, I shall describe a patient who decreased her sessions, initially with beneficial results and then a further decrease leading to a more disastrous situation; and also a patient who increased her sessions from once to three times weekly with apparently excellent results.

One question when considering frequency might be: 'How much intensity can this patient tolerate?'; another could be: 'What is the minimum degree of input that will help this patient to change through psychoanalytic work?'; a further question could be: 'What would be missed/not addressed in either too little or too much therapy?' and so on. There are no rules. Decisions will be based on innumerable factors in the patient but also on the thoughts and experience of the supervisor/supervisee dyad.

In contrast, where training and assessment are the determinants of the frequency of the work, there is more limited scope for consideration of frequency. Naturally, an assessment of an applicant as suitable does not necessarily mean that supervisors will agree, and in some cases supervisors (and more rarely trainees) will disagree with an assessment of suitability for training purposes – either on grounds of frequency, or on those of psychopathology.

I know that there is much dissent amongst supervisors and in the profession generally, in regard to consideration of frequency. Some consider those who are highly defended with poor reality sense more suitable for once weekly therapy, whereas others feel it is just such categories of patients who need more frequent sessions for the work to have impact. Where I feel I stand is that people at both extremes of the ego strength axis can be helped by once weekly therapy – i.e. how much or how little can they tolerate?

So, what kinds of patients might I consider as suitable for more frequent therapy? Some thoughts are:

• Those who want it and feel they need it.
• Where narcissistic issues predominate. I feel the therapist in once weekly therapy cannot have much impact on narcissistic personality structure, with all its terrors of intimacy and its powers of splitting, projective identification and hatred. 'These patients require an openly warm attitude from the analyst with a reasonable degree of involvement . . . analysts need to maintain their patients' feeling of connectedness with them . . .' (Cooper and Maxwell, 1995: 121).

- Where there is work to be done largely in the negative transference. As I quoted from my own experience, I find there is a need for more constancy and frequency in terms of sessions per week for effective work to be carried through in the negative transference.
- Where anxiety management and toleration of frustration are significant difficulties in the personality.

There is the question of what does 'more frequent' mean, if the work is not once weekly? Twice is different to thrice, which is different again from four or five times weekly. Ruth Barnett illustrates, in her 1992 paper, the move from two to three sessions, each increase having a particular impact for that particular patient.

Psychopathology of supervisee

It is perhaps stating the obvious to say that supervisees who are better analysed and more mature will work better with intimacy, dependency, regression, erotic issues, hatred, hopelessness and uselessness and be more able to identify their own feelings and fantasies in the therapy. Therefore, a supervisor needs to take careful account of the supervisee's blind spots and difficulties and, where appropriate, help the supervisee identify what needs to be taken to his or her own therapy. Training and assessment stir up paranoid fears and anxieties for us all.

How, then, would I assess suitability for intensive training? In particular, I am looking for non-rigidity of the personality and a capacity to learn. In his 1993 paper on supervision, Haesler warns of the difficulties in 'candidates who, because of specific aspects of their personality, show a tendency not to learn, to feel narcissistically wounded by being shown something they have not yet seen or reflected upon or that they do not yet know' (p. 550). Thus we are warned that an excess of narcissism in a trainee is likely to make for difficulties in supervision and the learning process.

Here is a brief example of a difficulty that was overcome in the supervisor/supervisee relationship. I once supervised someone in her psychotherapy training about whom I had serious concerns in terms of whether she had the personal qualities to become a good enough psychotherapist. I felt she was too rigid, too defended and too afraid of real intimacy with her patient. Our first six monthly assessment discussed some of these doubts, including a very stiff 'good morning' to my 'hello' each time she arrived for her session. Soon after, she told me that at the previous session when I had crossed my legs and pulled my skirt over my knees, it made a strong impact on her. She felt that she caused me to be 'stiff and covered up' with her, that she made me unrelaxed and embarrassed. If her supervisor had to cover up with her, what was she doing to her patients? This seemed to lead to some fruitful, in-depth exploration in her own therapy. Soon after, I began to notice a shift, a greater capacity to tolerate more personal communication and intimacy between herself and her training patients. Some time later, when she was approaching qualification, my doubts had largely abated and I was able to recommend her, as she had resolved and worked through many of the former difficulties.

Depth of work

I will take the 1995 paper by Gertrud Mander as my starting point. She illustrated from her first client that she 'learnt to hold her though periods of primitive rage, contain her high anxiety levels, survive her prolonged attacks on me in the transference, and work through a host of issues related to sexual and physical abuse in childhood'. She questioned 'whether a full analysis could have achieved more or quicker change and maturation . . .' (p. 5). If it is true that patients do as well in once weekly work, why do we train so intensively to see people three or even five times weekly? I feel I have both worked with myself and supervised patients who have made remarkable changes in once weekly therapy. However, I am not convinced that a once weekly session will significantly alter the areas of the personality where the deep-rooted psychotic anxieties lie, the envy and hatred dwell and the False Self predominates. For many patients once weekly therapy is sufficient to allow them to make choices and lead happier lives – which after all, as Jo Klein (1995) emphasises, should be the main aim of our work. For many, however, particularly those with narcissistic and borderline personality structures, more frequent sessions with the opportunity for more detailed investigation of the defences of the internal world; for more frequent 'connectedness'; for exploration of the minutiae of the transference/countertransference processes, may be the only hope of lasting structural, and thereby positive change. The patient I describe later who decreased her sessions to once weekly stopped making the gains that had hereto occurred in twice weekly sessions, whereas the patient who increased her sessions from once to three times weekly could certainly have continued to progress at the former frequency, but far more slowly.

Use of transference and countertransference

I know that transference and countertransference feelings in both therapist and patient can be very powerful indeed, whatever the frequency of the work. At the same time, however, the opportunity for the painstaking and detailed analysis and understanding of dreams, projections, identifications, defences and areas of projective identification as well as the degree of regression is clearly less available in 50 minutes per week.

Whether or not a patient's feelings are aroused to the same intensity is surely a matter for debate. I think that many might say that in a once weekly therapy the patient has to do more of the work him- or herself. That suggests the establishment of a strong working alliance, the internalisation of therapist as therapist rather than as transference object and makes regression much less likely.

In supervision of once weekly and more frequent work, understanding of the transference and subsequent working through of this is usually the nub of what we are struggling with. However, the nature of how we do this, what we interpret, how we say things, what we choose to tackle and what to overlook will vary considerably. It is one thing to offer something unpalatable, enraging or frightening to a patient who is being seen again very shortly (within a day or two), but it is another when the patient could have to carry this for a whole week. The degree of anxiety that a patient can tolerate would be assessed differently in once weekly as opposed to more frequent sessions.

Nature of the supervisory 'facilitating environment'

What then are the aims and duties of a good enough supervisor? Blomfield (1985) in his paper on 'Psychoanalytic supervision – an overview' lists a combination of education, an understanding of the psychoanalytic attitude and the use of the communicative relationship. The supervisor also has to 'study the complexities of the learning alliance' and focus on a sensitive clarification of the supervisee's countertransference, distinguishing between the patient's projections and the trainee's own emotional difficulties.

> The aim throughout is for the student . . . to develop his own style and sense of personal authority within a rigorous psychoanalytic framework. . . It is important all the time for the supervisor to be perfectly clear about the meaning *to the student* of the material provided by the patient. (Blomfield, 1985: 406)

Blomfield warns us about the danger of an insensitive supervisor conducting a monologue about the case, thinking all along that it was a dialogue. Throughout, this paper has emphasised 'negative capability', which Keats described as 'when a man is capable of being in uncertainties, mysteries, doubts, without any reaching after fact and reason'. This is what we are aiming for in ourselves and in our supervisees. Blomfield warns against the contrasting state identified by Keats when 'a Man who cannot feel he has a personal identity unless he has made up his Mind about everything . . . will never come at a truth as long as he lives;

because he is always trying at it' (Blomfield, 1985: 402).

Haesler's 1993 paper says much of the same. It looks at the position of the Supervisor between 'Teacher' and 'Analyst'. As Teacher we are trying to:

- teach how to listen
- point out blind spots in learning
- offer theoretical models in conceptualising
- help the supervisee to adopt the therapeutic stance of participant/observer.

As Analyst or Therapist we are trying to:

- help the supervisee's emotional responses and fantasies into the open
- help the supervisee with these feelings – love, hate, shame, etc.
- focus on the psychoanalytic encounter
- find blind spots within the material
- point to resistances in the case material in therapist and patient as well as in the supervisory relationship between supervisor and supervisee.

Blomfield emphasises 'constant self scrutiny', Haesler advocates permanent and careful review on the part of the supervisor as 'analyst to himself'. I believe this involves an attitude where there is no such thing as absolute 'psychic truth', which if it is held can be anything but facilitating to the supervisee. I once presented some case material in supervision and then again in a clinical seminar. My supervisor said 'you should have waited before interpreting', my seminar leader said 'you should have interpreted sooner'. I believe we have to eliminate the word 'should' from our supervisory vocabulary if we are going to offer our supervisees a 'maturational process and a facilitating environment' (Winnicott, 1976).

Clinical illustrations

I would now like to offer illustrations of supervision where the frequency of the sessions has changed and I shall quote from work with two supervisees.

Kathy and Jane

Jane was a second training patient for Kathy and, although her training requirement was for twice weekly, Kathy wanted to take another patient at three times weekly, and Jane herself seemed to accept this frequency. Her presenting problem was 'depression' and 'difficulty in sustaining relationships'. She also acknowledged that behind her confident and coping persona lay a growing sense of inner emptiness. For several months she saw Kathy three times weekly on three consecutive days. She would not use the couch, would outstare and verbally attack Kathy most of the time and made it clear that she experienced the therapy relationship as a battle for control, which she was determined to win. Kathy, in fact, felt that Jane was in charge most of the time, illustrated to her mostly because of a profoundly felt inability to think in the sessions. Jane told Kathy she saw her not as a person, but as a 'tape recorder' – i.e. as under her control, and not as separate or other. She was mostly contemptuous and denigrating of Kathy's links or interpretations and at the same time found silence unbearable. However, there was always a sense for me as supervisor that Jane found herself very needy of Kathy from the start and as the need and dependency increased, so did the attacks (a familiar scenario with borderline and narcissistic patients). After seven months of work, and the summer break, Jane found a job at a considerable distance from home and as a consequence reduced her sessions from thrice to twice weekly. This had some basis in reality, but was certainly felt by both Kathy and myself to be an unconscious attempt to protect herself from her neediness and an angry reaction to the summer break. Despite Kathy's valiant efforts to interpret this and hold the three times weekly frame that had been agreed, Jane was adamant, and the work proceeded at a frequency of twice weekly for a further 15 months, until more recently she dropped another session to once weekly. In fact, the work at twice weekly had become more thoughtful and productive. Jane gradually began, over time, to loosen her rigid defences, particularly those against vulnerability, certainty, lack of control, fear of Kathy's mind and Kathy's thinking capacities. The projective identification processes lessened to the degree that Kathy was allowed to think and feel, in response to Jane, and occasionally to sit with a few moments of silence. Jane continued to resist the couch fiercely, although her contempt and rudeness in relation to it abated. It is obvious that Jane managed glimmerings of trust towards Kathy, and the working alliance really only gained a hold after the move to twice weekly work.

Fifteen months after this move to twice weekly, however, Jane again changed her job and with the change came a reduction in salary. Over time, Jane had been getting increasingly into debt and now she became adamant that only once weekly sessions were possible – even though Kathy offered a reduction in fees. This occurred soon after the following summer break, and so again, but much more so this second time because the work and the awareness of need had deepened, Jane was full of rage, rebelling against the separation and Kathy's independent life. Then, in the autumn, Jane took a holiday herself and following this she clung to the idea that once weekly therapy was necessary and all that she could afford. She was in between jobs, in debt, still feeling unfulfilled in her personal relationships – yet it seemed to me and to Kathy that the breaks in the work and in their relationship were felt as intolerable by Jane. The only solution seemed to be to reduce her sessions. The defences she had managed to lower became raised again as she claimed that once weekly was the frequency that worked best for her. This was some months ago and this has clearly not proved to be so. Some of Kathy's frustrations have been vented in supervision and she says 'Layers of meaning are revealed in my mind in once weekly sessions, but there is no time now to work with them or work through them. We managed to keep the material alive in twice and three times weekly sessions, but now Jane's intention seems to be to bury it.' Kathy's difficulties in trying to keep the therapy alive at a frequency of once weekly, for this highly narcissistic patient are

- focusing on detail
- confronting
- finding enough space together to work anything through
- finding a way to understand all the denigration, denial and grandiosity.

She said, 'I find I am not working properly, I have to contain so much more and often find myself holding back if we reach painful material at the end of the session.' Jane spoke of a mother who 'delved into places I didn't want her to go' and this seems to explain why she is now clinging to once weekly sessions. She has found a way to continue to have her therapist on her terms.

The 'frame' has clearly been broken twice, both times through seemingly external circumstances but used to her own internal advantage. In fact, the reduction from three to two sessions weekly seemed to have been beneficial to the therapy. Jane made some progress – she became less persecuted by her therapist and more able to see her as trustworthy, a helpful figure who was not going to exploit her. But the next summer break seemed, certainly unconsciously, to have eroded some of these gains. In the once weekly work there are still glimpses of them: she has been able to say that she needs her sessions and that she needs Kathy to help her, but at another time she will virtually deny that this is so. The challenge now for Kathy and for me as her supervisor will be whether she can be helped back to twice weekly, whether she will take that risk. For Jane, the reduction to once weekly work seems to mean that she can be back in control and that ultimately being in control is what things are about. Unfortunately, if Kathy cannot help Jane to move with this, then I am not sure the impasse can be overcome.

Although I am well aware that once weekly sessions can be highly effective for many patients, I do think that for Jane 'more equals better' and I believe that Jane knows it too. The optimum frequency was discovered, by default perhaps, but it would seem to have been twice weekly.

In this case, as always, I as supervisor have had to bear in mind my roles as teacher and as therapist. Fortunately, I have with Kathy a good 'learning alliance', where she uses me well, trusts me and seems unafraid to open up and to confess what she feels are her 'mistakes' or omissions. She is frank about her emotional responses and her fantasies. In my role as 'supervisor as therapist' I have tried to understand with Kathy in what ways she may be blocking the process by current difficulties in her own emotional world, her 'blind spots', her increased vulnerability as she nears qualification and where unconsciously she may not be wanting such a difficult and demanding patient more than once weekly.

It is hoped that by making optimum use of my 'two supervisory positions', I will be able to help Kathy to move on with Jane.

Richard and Barbara

Barbara sought help, anxious about life following divorce and the departure of her children for further education. She was frightened of the prospect of life alone, wanting yet fearing to meet another partner. She asked for once weekly therapy for a limited time although it quickly became clear that was not what she wanted. It seemed like a protective device – in case Richard might not want her or like her. It very soon became evident that Barbara found it hard to deal with the gaps between sessions and indeed, she found the endings of sessions very difficult to accept, crying at the abruptness and being reminded of the death of a parent. The other parent is described as rigid and controlling. Richard soon proved to be elements of each – the one who either disappears or disapproves. The internal picture is of objects who are fragile and needy and those who are tyrannical. In the transference, Richard and Barbara alternate roles.

Besides finding the endings of the sessions and the gaps between sessions too much to bear, Barbara conveyed her neediness, a sense of loneliness and isolation and a hunger for more. There were references to this scattered throughout the material, including mention of a book title suggesting supplies might be short. Whilst we know that this material can be worked with (and frequently is) on the basis of once weekly sessions, and that a patient who is hungry and feeling unheld in once weekly work can experience exactly the same feelings (and almost certainly does) in three times weekly work, nevertheless, it seemed to me that this patient was begging Richard to be available to her more frequently. When he and I worked with this and then he offered it to the patient, she virtually lunged at it, confirming that perhaps this time the offer at least was the right food.

It took a couple of months to arrange this as she had to be assessed as a training patient; there were few doubts about entering into more intensive work, rather a sense of excitement. With this excitement were frissons of sexuality and Richard knew he would become involved in having to work with a good deal of erotic transference. He was frightened, yet excited too, as he knew it was an area where he felt relatively awkward and inexperienced. Four months after beginning once weekly work, at a time when initially the patient had safeguarded herself by saying she might leave and join a group, she entered into three times weekly therapy.

As predicted, the work quickly got into the area of erotic transference with Richard as her new 'partner' both at a fantasy level, but also referred to as such openly and jokingly by her children. It also produced talk of feeding on schedule as opposed to demand feeding, and Barbara's intolerance of the gaps increased. However, now the feelings could be explored more fully and really experienced. 'Excited but scared' were the feelings Barbara described in beginning three times weekly work. The same feelings exactly as Richard was experiencing, and to some degree, I too, in beginning to supervise a new training case.

Initially, Barbara found herself feeling fragile, tearful, wanting to withdraw and hide away in between sessions – in fact quite quickly more regressed as she also began to use the couch. She doubted whether Richard really wanted her or could take the full weight of her for three sessions each week – she felt grotesque and fearful that the increased frequency would make everything inside her erupt and she could no longer be held together.

She complained that her husband used to masturbate even though she and he still had intercourse. This seemed to be a warning to us that she feared that Richard with his training needs, or perhaps his eagerness to interpret, would prove to be the equivalence of masturbation. Would he also prove to be like her husband in perhaps getting her on to the couch for his own needs? In his position as the therapist behind the couch, he began to embody a parent who disappears and also a parent who may be felt to be disapproving, rigid and controlling. The transference was fast evolving, in all its infantile and erotic glory. I have illustrated from this therapy to try and show not only how differently Richard and Barbara were able to work when the frequency of sessions increased, but also Richard and I in our supervision sessions.

I am sure that much of this material would have evolved slowly over years of painstaking work at once weekly, and Richard and Barbara are still in the early stages of their relationship. Nevertheless, at a point in time where the material showed me and I could then show Richard how, unconsciously, Barbara kept pleading for more frequent supplies, Barbara was heard and understood with regard to her felt needs. If, in a case such as this, a patient is unable for whatever reason to take up the offer of more frequent sessions, then naturally the therapist works with the hunger, interprets the pain of the gaps and does one's best. All these issues are still present, but felt more intensely, I believe, in more frequent work. But at least we have the opportunity to be more closely with it and I think Barbara is safer to regress, to complain, to risk her sexual feelings.

Richard is entering new ground, particularly in regard to erotic transference and countertransference and I think, as well, with intimacy. Sometimes he is scared and tells me so, sometimes he resorts to theory as a reassurance and protection. His patient is also scared but enlivened by the new therapy, and she shows a preparedness and a willingness to enter as fully as she is yet able into the working alliance to discover what may emerge.

I am fortunate in that, in Richard, I have another supervisee with whom I have a good learning alliance. Richard is willing to take on board any perception we may get about his 'blind spots' and realises that sometimes he is shaky in his capacity for tolerating 'negative capability'. We have what feels like healthy debate about timing of interpretations, in particular with regard to interpretation of rage, and about waiting versus interpreting. His questions ensure that I constantly monitor what I am trying to do and my understanding of the patient/therapist interaction.

Unfortunately, Kathy feels somewhat of a failure in that her patient, initially three times weekly, is now coming once weekly, before a real significant change has taken place in her psychic structure. Richard, in contrast, feels pleased and to some degree satisfied, that his patient increased her sessions so readily, is working relatively well and is seeking intimacy, although also fearful of it. With each, at different times, I may be more 'teacher' or 'therapist' but always striving to discover what is needed and then to re-establish my supervisory balance between the two.

Conclusions: similarities and differences

I feel that, in many ways, this has been constantly addressed throughout this chapter. Our supervisory attitude needs to be virtually the same with whatever frequency patient the supervisee is bringing to us. Depending on what difficulties, technical or emotional he or she is undergoing, we may veer more towards 'teacher' or more towards 'therapist' for any period in time. Our self scrutiny needs to be in place (though in group supervision this can be helped somewhat by other members of the group). Many differences I have emphasised here are more between supervision during training and consultative supervision, irrespective of frequency of the sessions. I think where I need to be aware of the differences most acutely is in the type of interventions and interpretations that are appropriate at different frequencies. I would also say that, in general, more of everything is engendered in more frequent work – i.e. more hate, more love, more hopelessness, more dependency, more destructiveness. This means that *emotionally* there is more for the supervisee to contain and therefore more for the supervisor to contain. Gertrud Mander (1995) emphasises that once weekly work is different from more frequent work 'because of the need to make the hour memorable and meaningful for the clients' (p. 5).

I agree with this, which does not negate the differences and difficulties in more frequent work both in more emotional intensity and in issues of regression. Patients coming more frequently are more likely to make use of the couch. To my mind, supervising work with a patient on the couch is normally a very different experience from a face to face contact – as indeed those of us who have had therapy on the couch will be aware. As we saw from Richard's work with Barbara, attachment, erotic longings and regression quickly intensified. The supervisor needs to be fully aware of what kinds of anxieties and insecurities can be engendered in the therapist and to be attuned to what is needed in the supervisory sessions – possibly thinking in Kenneth Wright's terms of maternal and paternal modes of relating (Wright, 1991).

I shall draw to a close by saying that whilst I have tried to think about and explore the vicissitudes of supervision and in particular with regard to once versus more frequent work, the answer is that I do not know, I must stay with 'negative capability' – I cannot bring what Bion would call 'a brilliant, intelligent, knowledgeable light to bear' (1974: 37) on this difficult subject. However, I hope that this chapter has raised issues that will continue to be questioned and explored by others.

References

Barnett, R. (1992) Two or three sessions? *British Journal of Psychotherapy* 4: 430–41.

Bion, W.R. (1974) *Brazilian Lectures 1*. Rio de Janeiro: Imago Editora.

Blomfield, O.H.D. (1985) Psychoanalytic supervision – an overview. *International Review of Psychoanalysis* 12, 401–9.

Cooper, J. and Maxwell, N. (1995) *Narcissistic Wounds: Clinical Perspectives*. London: Whurr.

Haesler, L. (1993) Adequate distance in the relationship between supervisor and supervisee. *International Journal of Psycho-Analysis* 74: 547–55.

Jacobs, T. (1993) The inner experiences of the analyst: their contribution to the analytic process. *International Journal of Psycho-Analysis* 74: 7–14.

Killingmo, B. (1995) Affirmation in psychoanalysis. *International Journal of Psycho-Analysis* 76: 503–18.

Klein, J. (1995) *Doubts and Certainties in the Practice of Psychotherapy*. London: Karnac.

Mander, G. (1995) In praise of once-weekly work: making a virtue of necessity or treatment of choice? *British Journal of Psychotherapy* 12(1): 3–14.

Sandler, J. and Sandler, A.-M. (1978) On the development of object relationships and affects. *International Journal of Psycho-analysis* 59: 285–96.

Stimmel, B. (1995) Resistance to awareness of the supervisor's transference with special reference to the parallel process. *International Journal of Psycho-Analysis* 76: 609–18.

Winnicott, D.W. (1971) *Playing and Reality*. Harmondsworth: Penguin.

Winnicott, D.W. (1976) *The Maturational Processes and the Facilitating Environment*. London: Hogarth Press.

Wright, K. (1991) *Vision and Separation*. New York: Free Association Books.

Chapter 4
Dyads and triads: some thoughts on the nature of therapy supervision

GERTRUD MANDER

Supervision of psychotherapists has only recently become a subject of serious study. In the past, it was not acknowledged as a distinct professional activity that would deserve specific examination as to its processes, methods and products. There has been little interest in the question of what constitutes a supervisor as distinct from therapist or trainer, and for a long time the assumption was that any experienced therapist could give supervision, as if this was merely an extension of the therapeutic métier. The original name for the supervision of psychotherapists – control analysis – bears this out: it was seen as analysis with control, i.e. management and assessment added, as the supervision was of a trainee analyst's clinical work. Most of the literature is still concerned with training supervision and many fully trained therapists do not feel the need to continue in supervision, as they believe – surely naively – that self-supervision, like self-analysis, takes over after training supervision is finished.

The situation is changing and there is now vigorous research into many aspects of supervision and also the beginnings of an understanding that the supervisory task is in some ways more complex than therapy. It is certainly quite different from it in that the three-person field in which it operates requires from the practitioner a three-dimensional vision, an ability to observe and reflect on two or more relationships simultaneously, to link issues arising in one as a result of the other and to monitor a multiplicity of unconscious processes arising in the supervision field.

Theories of supervision

The classical statements on supervision were made by therapists who practised training supervision and observed a number of phenomena quite specific to that activity while in some ways analogous to therapeutic processes. H.F. Searles (1955), Ekstein and Wallerstein (1958) and Janet Mattinson (1975) examined their own reactions while supervising, and they discovered, in their countertransference, reflection processes in the supervisory relationship arising from the clinical material that was discussed. In addition to this observation which widened the emotional field of supervision, Mattinson became aware of, and focused on, the oedipal issues which become activated in the supervisee and patient and this enabled her to put her finger on a major difference between supervisor and therapist which needs to be examined further, a form of object-relating which is fundamentally different from the therapeutic stance.

Surprisingly, these issues are still largely neglected in the supervision practice of run-of-the-mill training supervisors, many of whom have not undergone a supervision training and hence have never felt the need to reflect on supervision *per se* or more specifically on their own method and style of practice. Thus hundreds of trainee therapists have had their cases supervised by supervisors surprisingly ignorant of what they were doing, who would probably have ranged themselves automatically alongside their supervisees' seminar leaders without further reflection on the specificities of their activity. Most of them would have exclusively focused on the transference and countertransference issues arising in their trainees' cases without giving much thought to what was going on in their own relationship with the trainee, as this was not considered relevant to the task or positively a hindrance to it. The trainee supervisees would have remained equally oblivious of it, colluding in the denial of their relationship as the supervisor's assessment was crucial to their professional development and success. The focus would have been firmly on either the patient and his or her transference and/or on the supervisee and his or her countertransference, with the supervisor routinely asking the latter what they felt (in order to gain more knowledge of the patient's problems) without considering that their own countertransference feelings and reactions to the supervisee's presentation might be of any or equal relevance, as, so the argument would run, this was not and definitely should not be a therapeutic relationship.

When, and if, the supervisee experienced strong feelings for and about the supervisor, this was a fact, but not a very welcome contribution to the ongoing activity. Hence hundreds of supervisors and supervisees never told their partners in the working relationship of their often quite intense emotional reactions in order not to dilute or hinder the task and turn into therapists/patients. In retrospect this seems extraordinary and a sad waste of opportunities comparable to the neglect of transference and countertransference phenomena in the therapies of earlier times. But not really surprising, considering how long it took before the emotional component in learning processes was included in investigations of these. Interestingly, Searles (1955/1986), who was probably the first to notice and identify the transference of unconscious communications from the patient to the supervisor via the therapist in situations where the latter remains impervious, ignorant or resistant to these, wrote his seminal chapter, 'The informational value of the supervisor's emotional experiences' (1955/1986) only a few years after Paula Heimann (1989) published her important paper on countertransference in 1949/50. He drew the logical conclusions from her remarks on the need to monitor and interpret the therapist's emotional reactions as an important part of the overall process, instead of ignoring or deploring them.

The merely pragmatic, blank-screen supervisor henceforth proved to be a useless myth as much as the blank-screen therapist who tried to efface himself and to ignore or suppress his emotions. It took the supervisory profession (which is only now becoming recognised as such) a long time, however, to take his observations to heart and there are still far too many practising supervisors who have not yet done this. The reason for this is probably a reluctance and fear of shouldering the full and immense complexity of the supervisory task which comprises much more material, more projective, introjective, identificatory, defensive, and persecutory processes when both relationships are taken into account and are properly analysed (as there are, of course, also unconscious transferences and resistances emanating from the supervisor and communicated to the patient via the therapist). Yet this reluctance saw a burden where there is an opportunity (not to say necessity) and overlooked the fact that here is a valuable tool that can lighten the burden considerably. This is not to say that the inclusion of the supervisor's countertransference and the use of what Searles called the reflection processes in supervision is an easy task, a magic formula or the open sesame of supervision that would deal effectively with the painful situation of not-knowing with which every supervisor is confronted in practically every supervisory session. But it was a momentous and wonderful discovery which adds not only to the interest but also to the usefulness and kudos of supervision.

Supervision under scrutiny – dyad and triad

Considering that 40 years have passed since Searles' important paper (and since Ekstein's and Wallerstein's (1958) observations on the learning problems of therapists) it is interesting that almost all clinical papers and theoretical discussions of therapeutic issues fail to include the contributions made by supervision to the success and progress made in psychotherapeutic work with patients. It feels like a conspiracy of silence, and certainly like a marginalisation of supervision, except in training. There is a practical reason for this, of course: publications are usually written by experienced therapists and experienced therapists are not in supervision, or if they are, they tend to describe their cases, as if this supervision had no meaningful influence on them. The exception is Patrick Casement (1985) who mentions in his book, *On Learning from the Patient*, his consultations with Winnicott and Paula Heimann over the problems of particular cases, but he does not advocate the practice of ongoing supervision for the experienced therapist as his notion of the 'internal supervisor' emphasises therapeutic autonomy. The training therapist, so the argument goes, internalises the training supervisor and draws on this internal good object, this benevolent professional super-ego to self-supervise the therapeutic processes on hand. This is, of course, imperative during the therapeutic session and Casement's notion of the internal supervisor and of trial identification with the patient (which, by the way, is not his own invention but an invention by, of all people, Wilhelm Fliess) is of utmost importance. But like all conscious, cognitive processes this 'island of intellectual contemplation' tends to get clouded over when the analytic space between therapist and patient fills up with anxieties, unconscious projections and the defences against these (employed by both partners in the relationship). Without an external supervisor it would not be possible in many cases to open up these complex and entangled processes for analytic understanding and the therapeutic couple will remain stuck – in the happy collusion of an erotic transference, the unhappy confrontation of a negative transference, the unproductive stalemate of an apparently unanalysable situation – when the therapist's capacity to think is temporarily, perhaps seriously, impaired and the internal supervisor is unable to operate with the necessary objectivity.

It would be interesting to conduct a study of how many therapists convicted of abusive conduct with their patients are in supervision, and hence abusing rather than using their supervisor. And how many are not, and hence are suspending or deceiving their internal supervisor, and believe that they have outgrown the need for a watchdog to keep them on the straight and narrow path of ethical therapeutic practice, to help them think about and analyse their relationships with their patients when they themselves are not fully aware, for whatever unconscious reasons, of what they are doing to or with them.

The argument is, *pace* Mattinson and Searles, that therapeutic dyads need to be opened up periodically to supervisory triads in order to function ethically and creatively, keeping alive the goal that the patient should become able to function autonomously and independent of the therapist. The obvious analogy is, of course, the development of the infant from the dependent dyadic relationship with the feeding mother to the increasingly more autonomous three- and multi-person relationships in the family with father and siblings, in society with peers, and with other authority figures. The supervisor might, for the sake of the argument, be seen as the father who, as Winnicott said, supports the mother/therapist in the effort to hold the baby/patient during the period of absolute dependence, of regression to dependence in the course of analytic therapy which may mobilise fusional and paranoid-schizoid defences in the patient or create powerful primitive, erotic and collusive transferences that can paralyse the supervisor-less therapist. As in the situation of the single mother who struggles to raise her child without the support of a partner and becomes the be-all and end-all for her child – both positively and negatively – the difficulty for the dyad is how and when to separate, how to establish firm enough boundaries of self- and not-self, how to survive idealisation and aggression, how to avoid abuse and, most important of all, how to live with and allow difference.

The mother who turns to her partner when the child has been put to bed steps out of her maternal preoccupation for a while, recovers her autonomous self and puts a temporary distance between herself and her baby in which she can think and reflect on their interaction, share her delights and her worries with another and prepare herself for another day of intense use by her child. A similar process happens between therapist and supervisor when they reflect on a clinical case. The outcome depends as much on the quality of their relationship – the transference and countertransference situation which operates between them – as with the parental couple. And the delight with which parents follow the progress of their baby equals the delight of supervisor and therapist when things develop well in a particular case. And the anxieties, when things don't go well, are comparable, too.

What matters is that there is space, analytic space, which the therapist can enter, and use as a safe container, a thinking base, a rehearsal stage, together with another, and where he or she can deliberately step outside the closed vessel of the therapeutic dyad, allowing a third person to look at the process. Winnicott's concept of the potential space, the intermediate area between mother and child in which their interaction – in health – is one of playful creativity, that lays the foundations for a child's healthy emotional development by carefully negotiating his narcissistic needs, has been used to describe the space in which good supervision takes place and where primary experience can be allowed to happen alongside the secondary processes of interpretation and reflection (Wilner, 1990). The problem with this understanding of supervision is that it conceives of it as a dyadic mode – as there are two people physically present in the room during the supervisory sessions, as in therapy. Yet these two people are there because of a third person, the patient, who influences what they are doing and thinking together. Searles, when observing his countertransference, extended the dyadic potential space to include the patient who, though not physically present, always enters and shares the emotional field when his clinical material is being discussed. Hence the potential space of supervision includes the therapeutic couple, and it is constantly concerned with problems arising in their relationship, otherwise it becomes therapy or teaching.

The supervisor is let into (or intrudes into) the couple's potential space. This is a risky business as inevitably resistance arises in the therapist and fear that the supervisor might take over the patient. This may lead to counter-resistance in the supervisor and to complications in the emotional field which can hinder or endanger the task in hand. There is thus a constant need to persuade the therapist of the value and safety of the supervisory container and an equally great need for the supervisor to guard against his or her own narcissistic needs to control, intrude and exclude.

In training, supervision is a compulsory procedure, involving the terrors of being judged and assessed, of competing with an expert and fearing to be found wanting. For the experienced therapist it can be a powerful challenge to their professional competence, to their unconscious need to stay in dyadic relationships and to their fear of exposure and vulnerability. To be found perhaps not to have been right or proper in one's professional conduct is always narcissistically wounding, and it leads to a temporary sense of uncertainty, shame and guilt. If so, it is the skilful supervisor's task to link the patient's material, his or her narcissistic needs, to what the therapist experiences, and to establish the unconscious parallel processes operating in the triangular field. One of the prime aims of good supervision is the aim of shaking the therapist out of complacency, omnipotence and comfortable certainty, and to provide a containing space where it is possible to bear uncertainty and admit mistakes. It is the prerequisite to learning and understanding something new (Szecsödy, 1990), it is a space where analytic thinking and linking can take place (Bion, 1967), where the therapist gains fresh insight first into what is going on between him or her and the patient, and ultimately what is going on in the patient's inner world in relation to his or her internal objects. When the supervisor can allow the supervisee to make their own discoveries in this process (from certainty to uncertainty to analytic insight) rather than spelling out his or her own thoughts and insights for them (didactically or authoritatively, which might be a narcissistic need of the supervisor), then supervision achieves what it has set out to do.

What matters is how the multiplicity of narcissistic needs operating in the triangular space as a result of analysing and working on the supervisee's therapeutic dilemmas is negotiated and understood. Like the 'good-enough' father who contains and supports the mother–baby dyad and helps the mother to be 'good enough' for her child – which means curbing and examining her narcissistic needs for satisfaction and for possessive love, and watching her envious and sadistic impulses, while allowing the child to give his needs and impulses full expression – the 'good-enough' supervisor supports, contains and at times challenges the therapist in order to help him or her be 'good enough' for the patient, whose growth and well-being is the main purpose of supervision as of therapy.

As in the dyad, in the triad there is the constant danger of one or the other participant slipping into behaviour that undermines the therapeutic and supervisory task, perverting or turning play and work into a sadistic power game, narcissistic gratification, or destructive sabotage of agreed contract and co-operation. The oedipal constellation, however, which revolves around issues of difference, differentiation, separation, relinquishment and rivalry, also allows for objectivity and distance, for standing a little apart, looking on rather than being fully involved in the subjectivity of pre-oedipal interaction which relies heavily on non-verbal unconscious communication and projection. The argument so far has been that the opening up of the therapeutic twosome to the supervisory threesome is necessary and salutary as it allows thinking, the planning of forward strategies and generally a relief from difficult unconscious stalemates.

Difficulties in the supervisory role

Objectivity, sustained observation and clear-headedness (not to be confused with intellectualisation or cleverness) are necessary qualities of the good supervisor, something achieved naturally perhaps in their emotional development or, more likely, with the help of a thorough and successful analysis. In the therapist, objectivity is a prerequisite too, but intuition, empathy, sensitivity and self-awareness may rank higher in importance. Objectivity is akin to self-lessness in the sense of not wanting something for oneself, e.g. wanting the patient, wanting to have all the insights, making all the interpretations. It means focusing on the objects and objectives out there without prejudice. In the supervisor it is a gift of seeing straight through the veils of projections, identifications and idealisations, of defences and resistance to the Gestalt of the interactive processes which are being reported by the therapist who has experienced them, while they are also being reflected in the emotional interaction of the supervisory couple. It is an ability to be inside and outside simultaneously, of participating and observing, at one remove from the therapeutic couple and yet being involved as a participant in the supervisory relationship.

When the supervisor's objectivity slips – overwhelmed, perhaps, by a desire to help (patient or therapist) or to teach and show off knowledge instead of allowing therapist and patient to find it, or by strong unconscious needs for love and admiration, by impulses like envy, anger, hate – the supervisor's warning bells should sound, either indicating a reflection process (which can then be made useful to the process) or something dangerously subjective, probably an unresolved oedipal problem of his or her own which is resonating from the past. If the supervisor is in supervision – a luxury which few supervisors allow themselves as yet but which should be considered a necessity by the truly scrupulous practitioner (particularly when no longer in personal therapy) – these matters can be worked through with the help of another. It happens all too easily that a supervisor gets drawn into taking over when the therapist appears or admits to stumble, into giving advice and being all-knowing and offering easy intellectual solutions when difficulties bristle on all sides. The temptations of power are never far away in an oedipal situation where the partners are of different quality and weight, more or less experienced, knowledgeable, intelligent, ruthless, greedy or needy.

The powerful supervisor comes in various guises: stern judge, strict parent, admired guru, laissez-faire friend, even ardent lover, all of which can do damage to, or impair the objectivity, playfulness and effectiveness of the supervisory process. Unless the supervisor remains on constant alert, examining his or her emotional responses, this activity can be counterproductive, abusive, and useless, and infect rather than elucidate the therapeutic activity which it is intended to benefit. In my opinion this makes supervision of supervision as necessary as supervision of therapy, but that, of course, adds another dimension to the ball-game, another relationship and another set of emotional responses . . .

The oedipal aspects of supervision

The argument is that the pull of unconscious forces in the three-person field of supervision is equally as powerful as in the two-person field of therapy, but that the issues are complicated by oedipal anxieties to do with inclusion and exclusion, jealousy, rivalry and competition. Janet Mattinson (1975) made this discovery in the course of a supervisors' workshop. The initially baffling reluctance of experienced supervisors to present their clinical work became entirely understandable when this was identified as resistance due to acute oedipal fears relating to exposure, jealousy and rivalry, and massive defences against these. This is borne out by Ekstein and Wallerstein's (1958) thorough study on the difficulties of learning in psychotherapy, though the authors did not address the oedipal aspects of their candidates' learning problems. It is also borne out by my own experience of training supervisors, where the supervision and assessment of their supervision is a central feature.

We noticed over the years how intense the competition is in the large group in which we teach and in the small groups in which we supervise. The trainees are unusually competitive with each other (or defending against it by being helpful), they are intensely critical of us tutors, and the anxiety levels are immensely high, while they also demand spoon-feeding. Students get intensely anxious when we make them supervise one another 'live' and assess one another's 'live' supervision in the presence of a tutor. Those who are experienced performers (teachers, trainers, actors) usually do best, as they have learned to live with their stage fright. Yet everybody admits to experiencing almost unbearable anxieties, even quite experienced supervisors, as Janet Mattinson (1975) found. She was the first to relate this to psychodynamic and developmental issues. The trainees defend against these anxieties in two ways – either by bending over backwards to be co-operative and helpful to each other, and then they avoid getting into negative or messy areas of the clinical material, or by becoming intensely rivalrous, preventing the supervising colleague from becoming active (when in the supervisee role), or by taking over the session and the patient (when in the supervisor role).

The anxieties affect the peer assessors too, and, to a lesser degree, the assessing tutor (who is assessing the supervision and the assessment of the supervision). Altogether a hothouse demonstration of oedipal anxieties in action, and of the defences against these – avoidance, abdication of authority, sadistic and offensive behaviour, seductiveness, compliance, and so on. All this is fed further by the reflection processes originating with any one of the three players on the supervisory stage, gripping the assessors and allowing the participant observer to study a complex panorama of anxieties, and of defences against these, which supervision generates, particularly when peer assessed and not yet fully mastered. Not surprisingly very few of the candidates manage, in this intensely competitive situation, to keep clearheaded enough to reflect on their own emotional responses and to think constructively across the whole field, and this usually impedes the full identification and interpretation of the reflection processes.

Add to this Janet Mattinson's (1975) concept of 'oedipal tangling', and the supervisory task proves its whole range of difficulties. Her emphasis on distance and difference as imperative to good supervision links up with the necessity of objectivity which was discussed earlier. ('Without distance there can be no difference, or, if there is too much similarity there can be only fusion', she states categorically.) But equally imperative is the capacity of the supervisor to survive 'oedipal tangling', to be flexible about the process of getting involved and relinquishing involvement which is an experience of constantly getting drawn into twosomes or intruding into twosomes, becoming an active participant of a 'tangle' while trying to retain the position of an observer.

The art of supervision is to remain flexible, to go in and to come out again, and to achieve and sustain an 'object relationship of the third kind' (after twosomes of love and hate) in which one can allow oneself to be a witness and relinquish the need to be a participant. 'Given this,

one can also be observed' says Ronald Britton (1989). There is a resolution to the Oedipus complex,

> if the link between the parents in love and hate can be tolerated in the child's
> mind . . . This provides us with a capacity for seeing ourselves in interaction
> with others and for entertaining another view whilst retaining our own, for
> reflecting on ourselves while being ourselves . . . The capacity to envisage a
> benign parental relationship influences the development of a space outside
> the self capable of being observed and thought about which is the basis for
> the belief in a secure and stable world.

Both the supervisee and the supervisor are constantly in need of this
space, of this capacity, which sustains the therapeutic alliance, the supervisory alliance, and the thinking work that influences the process.
Supervisors in particular have to be aware of their personal oedipal
issues – their need to establish special relationships, their competitive
anxieties, their separateness.

Allowing difference and holding distance, establishing and sustaining
a separate position, being able to bear the pain of exclusion and to overcome jealousy – these are the tasks to be mastered in the oedipal phase,
though mastery can never be fully achieved, as everybody's painful
experiences in supervision, and more generally in their life and love
relationships, prove. This stance requires an ability in the supervisor to
make quick choices as to where to focus during the presentation of clinical material. It also requires the supervisor to choose, in every individual instance, between being quite active or sitting back, trusting the
therapist's work with the patient or waiting for the moment when an
intervention is necessary and will be tolerated.

So far I have not mentioned group supervision in order to establish
clearly how I see the supervisory relationship by describing the three-
person model. Supervising in a group is in many ways more complicated than individual supervision as the dynamics of unconscious
group processes are also operative in the supervisory field, and these
add another dimension to the three-dimensionality outlined above.
Group supervision constantly throws up issues of sibling rivalry and the
basic-assumption defences of pairing, fight or flight which work heavily
against the performance of the task. When supervising in a group of
three (two supervisees, one supervisor) I first noticed the difficulty of
oedipal tangling, as inevitably one (or the other) supervisee demands
(or evokes) a special relationship with the supervisor. This situation
needs firm management, then it can be experienced as a goldmine of
parallel and reciprocal processes reflecting the clients' oedipal material.

Conclusion

In conclusion I want to stress once again that in supervision the model of object relations which is based on the dyad has to be augmented by a form of object relating which involves triads or multi-personal constellations in which quite different and distinctive problems and anxieties arise. Using Kleinian language it could be said that it is essential for the supervisor to have reached the depressive position, and developed the ability to identify and overcome instinctive and impulsive stirrings of jealousy, sadism and power in order to be effective. The likelihood that these stirrings are activated and intensified by issues arising from clinical material helps the supervisor in this task, as they can be made to serve the purpose of supporting the therapist and the patient in their work together. The identification and management of the supervisor's emotional responses is thus one of the fundamental components of good supervision, and it requires objectivity, self-awareness and rigorous thought, attitudes which are constantly under siege in a situation where the atmosphere is highly charged with unconscious processes affecting three or more persons in relationship to each other. Because of this I want to add a fourth requirement: vigilance. Closely linked to concentration and attentiveness this follows and facilitates the constant reflective processing of clinical material which constitutes the living process of supervision.

References

Bion, W. (1967) A theory of thinking. In *Second Thoughts*. London: Karnac.

Britton, R. (1989) The missing link: parental sexuality. In *The Oedipus Complex Today: Clinical Implications*. London: Karnac.

Casement, P. (1985) *On Learning from the Patient*. London: Tavistock.

Ekstein, R. and Wallerstein, R. (1958) *The Teaching and Learning of Psychotherapy*. New York: Basic Books.

Heimann, P. (1989) On countertransference. In *About Children and Children-No-Longer, Collected Papers 1942–80*. London: New Library of Psychoanalysis.

Mattinson, J. (1975) *The Reflection Process in Casework Supervision*. London: Tavistock.

Searles, H.F. (1955/1986) The informational value of the supervisor's emotional response. In *Collected Papers in Schizophrenia and Related Subjects*. London: Karnac.

Szecsödy, I. (1990) Supervision: A didactic or mutative situation. *Psychoanalytic Psychotherapy* 4(3): 245–61.

Wilner, W. (1990) The use of primary experience in the supervisory process. In *Psychoanalytic Approaches to Supervision*. Current Issues in Psychoanalytic Practice (ed. R.C. Lane), Monographs of the Society for Psychoanalytic Training No. 2. New York: Brunner/Mazel.

Chapter 5
Solitude and solidarity: a philosophy of supervision

DAVID HENDERSON

> The small hermit lives on a mountain. The great hermit lives in a town.
> Chinese saying (Porter, 1993)

In this chapter I will outline my philosophy of supervision. This is centred on the identity of the therapist. I have in mind a therapist in private practice working with individuals in open-ended analytical psychotherapy. The focus is on the 'deep' background of supervision rather than the foreground. Therefore, there will not be space to consider technical issues of supervision in detail. There will also be no attention given to group supervision or the institutional setting of supervision. These are interesting and important issues, but I devote myself here to trying to clarify the archetypal roots of the sense of vocation.

Locating the analytic vocation

The practice of analytic psychotherapy is a vocation that is an expression of an archetypal impulse. This impulse is fundamentally impersonal, being rooted in the collective unconscious. A vocation is a way of life that embodies and particularises an archetypal imperative. As a therapist develops and matures in his or her practice this impersonal potential comes to be expressed in a unique way which in turn contributes new possibilities to the collective image.

Analytic psychotherapy is an expression of the Healing archetype. Archetypes are verbs – they are alive. They manifest in human nature as actions or images. The aim of the Healing archetype is to repair, mend, renew, restore. According to analytical psychology we experience archetypes as having two poles, material and spiritual. At the material end of the spectrum with this archetype we find forms of medicine, house restoration, disaster relief, motor mechanics, trouble-shooting, darning socks, etc. In nature we witness the incredible capacity of the body and ecosystems to heal given the right conditions.

The spiritual end of the spectrum is expressed in the search for meaning, emotional or psychological healing, understanding, and soul or spirit experience. I believe that the Shaman is the original expression of this pole of the archetypal intent in human society, but that over time some aspects of the Shaman's identity have split off and developed a character and autonomy of their own. I now see two streams of activity flowing from the spiritual aspect of the healing archetype – the shamanistic and the contemplative.

The lists in Table 5.1 are an attempt to evoke these two currents of values, activity and modes of consciousness.

Psychotherapists are often seen to have taken over the role of the priests: to be priests for a secular age (Jung, 1933; Rieff, 1966). To my mind the identity of the analytic psychotherapist is closer to that of the Hermit than the Priest. The Analyst is the descendent of the Hermit. They are expressions of the same archetypal impulse.

The image of the Analyst informs the practice, understanding and identity of the psychodynamic psychotherapist in the same way that the image of the Hermit informs monastic life. Just as few psychodynamic counsellors or therapists become analysts, few monks become hermits. However, when the therapist is practising psychotherapy he or she embodies this particular archetypal potential, even though other aspects of the therapist's life may be informed by very different demands.

Elements of the archetype

I will now explore eight elements of the Hermit identity or image: Solitude, Humility, Liminality, Ecstasy, Craft, Shame, Kindness and Zeal. These are fundamental values, energies, potentials or intentions. They are of course elements of every human life but have a distinct constellation in the life of the hermit and the analytic psychotherapist.

Table 5.1 Shamanistic and contemplative streams of activity

Shamanistic	Contemplative
Priest	Hermit/monk
Humanistic psychology	Analytic psychotherapy
Public	Private
Mythological	Symbolic
Transpersonal	Alchemical
Catophatic	Apophatic
Performing arts	Fine arts

According to Searles, 'the patient is ill because, and to the degree that, his own psychotherapeutic strivings have been subjected to such vicissitudes that they have been rendered inordinately intense, frustrated of fulfilment or even acknowledgement' (Searles, 1979). I would suggest that those clients benefit most from analytic therapy who have a particular need to discover, humanise or understand their 'psychotherapeutic strivings' in the areas of the eight qualities mentioned above. This could have consequences for assessment for analytic therapy and for selection of trainees.

In the following impressionistic sketches of each of the eight elements of the Hermit image, A refers to the Hermit, B to the therapist and C to the therapist's shadow.

Solitude

A The most immediate association with the Hermit. They practise physical and spiritual solitude. 'Alone with the Alone' (Plotinus). They leave the world and, in some traditions, the self behind. Father Moses of Skete, a Desert Father, said: 'Go sit in your cell and your cell will teach you everything' (Merton, 1960). Shunryu Suzuki, a Japanese Zen master, said: 'Do not think about anything. Just remain on your cushion without expecting anything. Then eventually you will resume your own true nature. That is to say, your own true nature resumes itself' (Suzuki, 1970). Living in deserts, mountains, caves, forests, cloisters.

B For Winnicott the True Self is in a profound sense unknown, but is seen through the 'spontaneous gesture' (see Phillips, 1988). For Jung, 'The man whom we can with justice call "modern" is solitary' (Jung, 1933). Therapists can spend many hours each week alone with clients. The therapist stays within the cloister of the analytic attitude or container. This involves leaving behind attitudes, preoccupations and needs that are inappropriate to the setting and work. Confidentiality is a type of solitude. The remedy for the failure of analysis is more analysis.

C Gossip. Being hungry for clients' visits. Endless training as an escape from being in one's own place. Restlessness.

Humility

A Humility, from the same root as humus, points to the earth. In the Rule of St Benedict humility is the sign of the true monk. It is the acknowledgement of one's proper relationship with others, with nature and with God. 'Bowing is a very serious practice. You should be prepared to bow, even in your last moment . . . Our true nature wants us to . . . A Master who cannot bow to his disciples cannot bow to the Buddha' (Suzuki, 1970). Hospitality, Simplicity.

B Recognition of dependency. Awareness of limitations, pathology, inflation, projection, envy, greed, etc. Honouring the potential of the client. Reality principle. Depressive position. Stage of concern.

C Humiliating clients by rubbing their noses in it. Lack of imagination. Stuck. Prosaic.

Liminality

A Edges of towns or fringes of civilisations. Ambiguous relationship with religious communities, political authorities. Hospitable but difficult to reach.

B Cusp of art and science, conscious/unconscious, inner/outer. Ambiguous relationship with client's 'real life' and with political/medical/cultural establishment.

C Lust for professional security. Seeking security by forcing oneself into the centre of the client's world by aggressive transference interpretation.

Ecstasy

A Standing outside one's self. Clairvoyance, telepathy, 'prayer of fire', kundalini. Journeying in psychic world, planes of consciousness. Sexual and psychospiritual energies. Tantric practices.

B Theory and theorising. Countertransference. Empathy. Seeing the client's potential.

C Esoteric or ungrounded interpretations. Teaching the client. Sex with client.

Craft

A The Desert Fathers wove baskets. Ryokan, a Japanese hermit, was a poet. Chinese hermits were political theorists, herbalists, painters, gardeners. Carthusian hermits each have their own workshop.

B Attention to technique. Management, note-taking, history-taking. Skilful use of interventions.

C Pedantic. Textbook interpretations.

Shame (sorrow)

A 'What the Greeks call "accidia" which we may term weariness and distress of heart . . . dejection and, especially trying to solitaries, and a dangerous and frequent foe of dwellers in the desert' (Cassian, 1978). 'Perfect correspondence to his grace consists in a strong deep interior sorrow . . . Every man has plenty of cause for sorrow but he alone understands the deep universal reason for sorrow who experiences *that he is* ... He alone feels authentic sorrow who realises not only *what he is* but *that he is* ... occupied and filled with a foul stinking lump of himself ... he almost despairs for the sorrow that he feels, weeping, lamenting, writhing, cursing and blaming himself' (Johnston, 1973). Flagellation, austerities, fasting. 'Gift of tears'.

B Tragic view of life. Kleinian obsession with envy. Classical Jungian obsession with the shadow. Being a receptacle for the misery and shame of clients. Constant contemplation of the insufficiency of the ego. Shame as a natural emotion when the ego reaches its limit before truth or beauty. Fear of the unknown. Paranoid (shameful) prelude to depressive position (humility).

C Cynicism, hopelessness. Contempt for clients and other therapists. Paranoia. Bullying and beating clients with interpretations. Desperation about professional prestige. Sadomasochistic sex with clients.

Kindness

A Not niceness, but recognition of kinship – we are the same sort of creatures, from the same source. The Buddhist concern for all sentient beings. Hospitality. Not judging. St Francis preaching to the birds.

B Empathy. Compassion. Countertransference. Training analysis. Acceptance.

C Nicey-nice. Oversolicitousness. Inappropriate disclosure – 'when that happened to me'. Over-identification with client. Being too soft.

Zeal (courage, ruthlessness)

A The Guardians of the four directions at Buddhist temples are frightening statues, armed figures to protect the inner temple. Exorcism. The gatekeeper sending the postulant away, the postulant perservering – both ruthless. Confronting demons. Seeing through Maya (illusion).

B Holding the boundaries. Confrontation. Naming negative transference. Guardian of the analytic space, alchemical vessel (Field, 1990; Hillman, in Moore, 1989).

C Unbending. Too demanding. Rigid, defensive, blocking the client out. Uncontrolled use of insight and confrontation – a cutting assault on the client. Not allowing client into the space/relationship. Penetrating the client in a triumphant way.

I feel that the most problematic elements for individual therapists in the current cultural climate are Solitude and Shame. With the heavy emphasis in theory and in the media on relationships, the idea of Solitude is pathologised or seen as a failure. There is also a tendency in theory to pathologise deep unshakeable sorrow and shame rather than to reflect on ways in which they may be a natural human inheritance. The feel-good factor is highly valued in the culture and the economy. In an entrepreneurial or new age environment it can be hard for the individual therapist to sit with his or her own shame and sorrow as well as that of the client and the disowned shame of the culture and profession.

On the level of the psychotherapy profession there is a good deal of ambivalence about Liminality. It seems to me that at least some of the anxiety about accreditation is due to fear of this quality. However, where psychotherapy becomes too secure or respected it can lose something vital (through over-identification with the Mother and Father archetypes?). To what degree is the pressure for statutory regulation of psychotherapy an attempt to escape Liminality? What are the dangers of this move?

The supervisor/supervisee relationship

The supervisor/supervisee relationship is the environment for the deintegration/reintegration of the archetypal potential in the Hermit image. This process is largely unconscious. On a conscious level a great deal of attention is devoted to management (Craft) and theory (Ecstasy) and most theories of supervision focus on these elements. However, a supervisor who can hold in view the full constellation of the image will have more freedom in adapting to situations where other elements are at issue.

The supervisee's own therapy is rightly given a certain pride of place in training and beyond qualification. However, this is usually at the expense of a proper understanding and valuing of the role of the supervisor. In his or her own therapy the supervisee is client, patient, infant, child, etc. In supervision the supervisee presents himself or herself specifically as a *therapist*. This means that these archetypal issues are most focused and intense in relation to the supervisor (more so even than when working with an individual client).

The projection of this therapist/Hermit identity on to the supervisor can be extremely potent. It seems to me a real failure of nerve and vision to reduce these powerful, primitive projections solely to parental/developmental issues. The understanding of the relationship in developmental terms is vital, but inadequate as an overall philosophy. While it is true that these archetypal potentials have been deintegrated/reintegrated in relation to parents, siblings, teachers, therapists, books, institutions and buildings, in the supervisor they find their most coherent object.

Anthony Stevens has written about the 'frustration of the archetypal intent' (Stevens, 1982) in relation to the Mother and Father archetypes. I find it useful to think of failures in the supervision relationship (and the consequences of these for the client) as frustrations of the archetypal intent of the Hermit. The love and hate involved in this projection can be as powerful as in parental projections, because what is being projected is at the core of the supervisee's life purpose. The drive to find vocational fulfilment (will to meaning) can be ruthless.

In my own experience I have had difficult relationships with supervisors. One was not at peace with his own Shame so he 'beat' me by constantly telling me that I was clinically depressed and needed therapy at least twice a day, adding that he imagined I had no friends. (This was also a failure to grasp the reflection process since he was treating me the way my client's father had treated her.) Another supervisor was addicted to Ecstasy. He made brilliant intuitive statements about my clients but was seemingly unable or unwilling to enter into the nitty-gritty of my relationship with them, as though he did not want to get his feet dirty.

Because the supervisor/supervisee relationship is the locus of such profound meaning for the supervisee I think that it can be as important to a therapist as his or her own therapy. One way of fending off the intensity of this demand on both parties is to draw exaggerated distinctions between supervision and therapy. One area where supervision suffers in this division of labour, it seems to me, is in the full disclosure of countertransference. Supervisees find it dangerous to disclose countertransference because it is a vulnerable thing to do, but also because many supervisors do not want to hear. Supervisors can be frightened (for personal or professional reasons) of getting involved with their supervisees at the depth that the archetypal imperative is demanding. Instead, supervision is often seen as an 'interesting' addition to one's case load. It is worth remembering, however, that while supervision is not therapy it is an analytic relationship with the potential to damage or nurture the vocational aspirations of both participants.

The fate of the object (client)

Daniel Stern has drawn the distinction between the observed infant and the clinical infant. The former is an actual infant whose behaviour is observed by the developmental psychologist. The clinical infant is a 'recreated infant made up of memories, present re-enactments in the transference and theoretically guided interpretations' (Stern, 1985). I see an analogous relationship between the observed client and the clinical client. The observed client is the client that the supervisee knows in the therapy session. The clinical client is the client recreated in the supervision session.

The supervisor and supervisee engage in an analysis of the clinical client which includes consideration of verbatum reports, experimentation with different theoretical models, attention to the transference/countertransference as reported by the supervisee and as experienced in the supervision relationship. The work enables the supervisee to build up an understanding of the relationship between the observed client and the clinical client.

Central to the business of supervision is the recognition of ways in which the supervisee has become identified with the client, especially where these identifications create blind spots, threaten to undermine the therapy or lead to acting out, recreate abusive or collusive object-relating, or threaten the physical or mental health of the supervisee. By becoming conscious of these identifications the supervisee can see the client more clearly and can return to himself or herself.

It follows from the first part of this chapter that these identifications have very different meanings for the client and the supervisee. A client will experience, consciously and unconsciously, the process of therapy as one of deintegration/reintegration of a wide range of feelings, memories, part-objects, images, etc. from his or her past, present and future. For the supervisee the identifications cluster around the elements of the vocation discussed earlier. My image is that each element of the Hermit image acts as a magnet that attracts different bits of the client's psyche – like iron filings. The supervisor must bear in mind the personal meanings of this identification for the client, as well as the meaning for the supervisee's vocational identity.

So, for example, a part-object relating to the client's relationship with the mother – say an aspect of oral sadism – may attach itself to Zeal in the supervisee's inner world. It is a relief for the client to have the part-object contained by the supervisee and returned to the client in some type of conscious or unconscious interpretation. It is a relief for the supervisee to have this capacity for Zeal used by the client and consciously or unconsciously acknowledged by the supervisor.

The danger of viewing these identifications from the supervisee's side solely in terms of personal development issues is that this does not recognise the essentially impersonal root of the supervisee's identity as a therapist. The supervisee needs to come to terms with the impersonal demands of his or her vocation and learn how to be objective about his or her own experience of the elements of the archetypal image. The supervisee needs to develop faith in the fact that these elements are operating within his or her personality in an autonomous way that can be relied upon to do the job.

There are therapists who, despite a good deal of analysis, training and supervision, have an extremely fragile sense of vocational identity. They do not seem to be in possession of their own authority and autonomy as therapists. My understanding of this is that they have not yet found their right relationship with the archetypal aspects of the identity. A therapist who has this foundation will be comfortable and secure dwelling in the solitude of the analytic container. This type of therapist will be happy to receive clients or be used by clients and will not be too distressed when clients leave. He or she provides the client with the space to grieve, fight, suffer and play.

I feel that the supervisor's first duty is to the analytic container, second to the supervisee and third to the client. This ensures that the client actually gets something useful. In terms of supervision, the fate of the client is dependent upon the capacity of the supervisor to see the supervisee as a therapist and to confirm that identity, an identity they share at the level of the archeypal image.

Conclusion

In this chapter I have tried to clarify the archetypal roots of the analytic psychotherapist's vocation: that it is an expression of the archetype of Healing, mediated through the Hermit image. The supervisor/supervisee relationship is the place where this identity is most comprehensively evoked, challenged, confirmed and strengthened. The elements of Hermit image (Solitude, Humility, Liminality, Ecstasy, Craft, Shame, Kindness and Zeal) are universal, but have a distinct constellation in this image. A therapist who is in tune with the archetypal imperative in these elements will be able to provide a setting in which the client's 'true nature resumes itself' (Suzuki, 1970).

My solitude, however, is not my own, for I see now how much it belongs to them – and that I have a responsibility for it in their regard, not just in my own. It is because I am one with them that I owe it to them to be alone, and when I am alone they are not 'they' but my own self. There are no strangers! Thomas Merton (1966)

References and further reading

Cassian, J. (1978) Institutes and conferences. In *The Nicene and Post-Nicene Fathers*, Vol. II. Kalamazoo, MI: Eerdmans.

De Board, R. (1978) *The Psychoanalysis of Organisations*. London: Tavistock.

Ekstein, R. and Wallerstein, R. (1958) *The Teaching and Learning of Psychotherapy*. New York: Basic Books.

Field, N. (1990) Healing, exorcism and object relations theory. *British Journal of Psychotherapy* 6(3): 274–84.

Greenson, R.R. (1991) *The Technique and Practice of Psycho-Analysis*. London: Hogarth Press.

Hawkins, P. and Shohet, R. (1989) *Supervision in the Helping Professions*. Buckingham: Open University Press.

Johnston, W. (transl.) (1973) *The Cloud of Unknowing*. Garden City, NJ: Doubleday.

Jung, C.G. (1933) *Modern Man in Search of a Soul*. New York: Harcourt Brace Jovanovich.

Kaslow, F. (ed.) (1986) *Supervision and Training: Models, Dilemmas and Challenges*. New York: Haworth Press.

Lane, R. (ed.) (1990) *Psychoanalytic Approaches to Supervision*. Current Issues in Psychoanalytic Practice (ed. R.C. Lane), Monographs of the Society for Psychoanalytic Training No. 2. New York: Brunner/Mazel.

Mattison, J. (1992) *The Reflection Process in Casework Supervision*. London: Tavistock Institute of Marital Studies.

Merton, T. (1960) *The Wisdom of the Desert*. New York: New Directions.

Merton, T. (1966) *Conjectures of a Guilty Bystander*. Garden City, NJ: Doubleday.

Moore, T. (ed.) (1989) *A Blue Fire: Selected Writings by James Hillman*. New York: HarperCollins.

Phillips, A. (1988) *Winnicott*. London: Fontana.

Plaut, A., Dreifuss, G. and Fordham, A. (1982) Symposium: How do I assess progress in supervision? *Journal of Analytical Psychology* 27, 105–30.

Porter, B. (1993) *Road to Heaven: Encounters with Chinese Hermits*. San Francisco: Mercury House.

Rieff, P. (1966) *The Triumph of the Therapeutic*. Harmondsworth: Penguin.

Searles, H. (1965) *Collected Papers on Schizophrenia and Related Subjects*. London: Hogarth Press.

Searles, H. (1979) *Countertransference and Related Subjects*. New York: International Universities Press.

Stern, D. (1985) *The Interpersonal World of the Infant*. New York: Basic Books.

Stevens, A. (1982) *Archetypes*. New York: William Morrow.

Suzuki, S. (1970) *Zen Mind, Beginner's Mind*. New York: Wetherill.

Weiss, S.S. (ed.) (1987) *The Teaching and Learning of Psychoanalysis: Selected Papers of Joan Fleming, MD*. New York: Guilford Press.

William of St Thierry (1980) *The Golden Epistle*. Kalamazoo MI: Cistercian Publications.

Chapter 6
Super vision:
seen, sought and
re viewed

HERBERT HAHN

The good, the bad – and the ugly?

This is a paper about how I first *saw* supervision as a supervisee; sought further understanding in the literature; and researched and reviewed my own work as a supervisor in dialogue with some supervisees. This whole process did not proceed in chronological order. Indeed, I had already written a draft paper on supervision for presentation at Limbus in Devon, when I came across a paper by Barbara Stimmel (1995). In it she convincingly emphasised the importance of the supervisor doing self-analytic work on his or her own *transference*, as well as countertransference. Her paper gave me a useful nudge to research. Similarly responses by supervisees to my notes led to further reflection.

Some 30 years ago I was a keen young trainee child psychotherapist at the Tavistock Clinic. As memory recalls – my subjective memory, that is – supervision worked like this: the established and highly acclaimed senior clinician who was my supervisor ordered me to produce detailed process notes, which I was to read verbatim. (She didn't actually order me, but advice coming from such a height felt like an order.)

As I read, the supervisor stopped me from time to time when she was ready to interpret what I was reading as if it was coming directly from my patient. I was very impressed by her deep interpretations, which seemed so much better than anything I had been able to think of. Sometimes I was so impressed that I even tried to reproduce her interpretations in subsequent sessions with my patient. Occasionally I would be asked by my supervisor what my *countertransference* was. By this question I was frequently flummoxed. For one thing I was waiting anxiously for my supervisor's next interpretation of my material; and for another I mistakenly thought that by countertransference she meant some profound insight buried deep in my unconscious and which I did not know how to reach. Only after this relationship ended did I come to realise that my relationship with my supervisor had been fraught with idealisation to the detriment of my own and my patient's development.

Some years later, quite by chance, I met someone who trained soon after me and we discovered we had worked with the same supervisor: he told me that one day she had left the room in the midst of a session. Overcome by curiosity, he had taken the opportunity to peek at the notes she had been making during the supervision. He discovered that she had recorded almost everything he had been reading to her about his patient's communications, but nothing at all about what he had said to his patient. This was a shock to me. On reflection, I wondered whether the supervisor's method of supervision might have included a need to show how brilliant she was. This may have had deleterious effects on my own confidence; and to the extent that I identified with this role model, my patient might have been similarly adversely affected.

Within my training context at that time, supervision was considered to be of vastly secondary importance to analysis direct and all accredited training therapists were assumed to be competent as supervisors. Indeed, the supervisor I have referred to had a very good reputation as a therapist and none of us would have dared question whether she might nevertheless be doing a poor job with her supervisees. She herself would also have been offered no training or support for this task. Thus when I read Oberman's (1990) account of instances where supervision failed, even when gifted students were being supervised by skilled and experienced analysts; he was for me like the little boy who had the courage to exclaim on the nakedness of a royal personage.

It will not surprise you to hear that when I came to take on the role of supervisor myself, I discovered that it was much easier to be critical of a particular supervisor, than to know how to do a good enough job myself. Indeed it became all too clear that the supervisor's task is highly complex. To quote Clarkson (see Chapter 10)

> At any one moment of time, any supervisor may need to be a Cerberus guarding the territories and boundaries . . . a Psyche-sorter of the wheat and barley of primary and secondary realities. . . a Zeus-like referee between internal and external factions. . . a Chironic mentor teaching and modelling the skills of healing . . . a Hestian flame . . .

of the spirit of the profession.

In recent times, led by initiatives in the counselling profession, numerous endeavours have been made to address supervision as a task in its own right. For example, Crick (1992) consulted supervisees about their views on the difference between good and bad supervision. She learned that after a session with a good supervisor, supervisees felt better able to understand previously elusive aspects of the therapeutic process. By contrast, the effect of a 'bad' supervision was to leave the supervisee feeling burdened with the responsibility of coping with the supervisor's views as well as the patient's. Bad supervisors tended to be experienced as narcissistic and competitive or as using 'not knowing' or 'uncertainty' in an idealised way so that 'proper attempts to strive to know' were inhibited (p. 242).

In Barbara Stimmel's (1995) paper, she illustrates from her own work the importance of supervisors monitoring personal *unconscious transferences*, as well as countertransferences to supervisees. She warns that supervisors are at risk of self defensively exploiting useful notions such as parallel process as a way of not confronting themselves. By way of example, she relates that she explored self-analytically a difficulty in her work with a black supervisee. At first she considered that this may have been due to her unconscious racism. With further self-analytic work, she discovered that what looked like her racism hinged more deeply on her unconscious rivalry with her supervisee. She concludes that the difficulty in this supervision was the responsibility of the supervisor involving 'my resistance against a more complete confrontation with myself' (Stimmel, personal communication).

Basil Smith (1994) developed a similar theme, exploring supervisors' and supervisees' phantasies about each other. He found that at an unconscious level a supervisee can experience the supervisor as 'the tyrant who knows it all; the secret therapist; or, the agent of the training committee'. The supervisor, on the other hand, may be harbouring envious or rivalrous phantasies towards the supervisee or towards the supervisee's therapist.

One might add that the supervisor may also narcissistically require the supervisee to do *brilliantly* with the patient. In bad supervision supervisors unconsciously project their own difficulties via the unconscious of their supervisees, into the patients of those supervisees (Clarkson, personal communication) – the parallel process operating in reverse!

Good enough supervision

Exploration of the shadow side of supervision need in no way deter us from celebrating the value of good and also 'good enough' supervision, bearing in mind that individual needs vary and change and that there can often be healthy confrontations in the supervisory relationships, out of which new and better ways of working together emerge. However, the balance of power and responsibility lies on the side of the supervisor, hence the importance of Stimmel's thesis. Smith, among others, objects to being labelled a SUPERvisor – someone who can see in a super or superior way – who supposedly has metaphorically grown a Third Eye. However, Y.T. Tsegos (1995) suggests that the image of the Third Eye for the supervisory process can be taken to refer to 'something deeper and more enriched which emerges in the *matrix* of the supervision session' (p. 119). Tsegos is explicitly referring to group supervision, but I do think the same principle applies to dyadic work, where the matrix may be understood as the facilitating (but also potentially debilitating) environment of the supervisory encounter which will hopefully encourage assimilation, containment and discovery, but may also be collusive, destructive and disabling. The supervisory relationship may be analogous to that of a parental couple in dialogue about a child, with the parent who has been away at work advising the one who is the primary care giver. They may co-operate to reach a deeper understanding of the child, in which the caregiver feels supported and gains further confidence, or they may collude in a way which is destructive and may even become abusive.

Case material

Helen

At our first meeting Helen seemed apprehensive and revealed that it was only after quite a long period of personal therapy that she could now consider having supervision with a man. She went on to outline her work context, but was very unforthcoming about herself. In subsequent sessions we would sometimes mutually engage in focusing on her work. However, she often gave outlines of 'problems', seeming to hand them over to me to solve. I found it difficult to draw her out; as if what she was saying was so obvious as not to require elaboration, yet I felt I had very little to go on. I had a sense that she felt somewhat oppressed by her work, yet it was not on her agenda to acknowledge this openly with me. Instead overtly she bombarded me with requests for practical solutions. Sometimes when I responded with anything other than a direct suggestion, and offered my thoughts or hypotheses about the work situations she sketched, she ignored what was offered and continued to speak as if these ideas had no relevance. Typically, then my own response, in turn, was to feel I was failing her and that I needed to 'try harder'; I would find myself offering her more and more – but with no apparent effect. The supervision sessions themselves sometimes felt oppressive, and I did not always look forward to them. Although I was aware of these feelings and of a degree of tension in the relationship between us, I somehow did not feel it would be at all 'safe' to talk about this; that this would be too threatening to her; and it was my job to 'contain' the disease I was experiencing. We continued with regular meetings for quite a time, but eventually we agreed to call a halt. In our last session, we reviewed our experience with each other. I then learned, to my surprise, that Helen had come to me for supervision with an assumption that I would not take her work seriously no matter how perfectly she presented it. Further, in order to approach her supervision with me 'properly' she had been very careful to talk to me only about her work itself, and reserve all of her own feelings, even if they related to her work, for her personal therapy. She had expected me to be like her father who looked down on women and their feelings.

Helen also asked me how I had found working with her. I said that I had found it interesting to work with her and been impressed by how seriously she took her work; that I had also struggled at times when I felt that she did not find what I offered her as useful, and that my thinking about this and trying harder did not seem to help.

Helen then responded with surprise and relief. Surprise, that I had actually thought about her and her needs; and relief that I too had had a struggle.

After we had stopped, and I had written up these notes, I further reflected on my experience of the supervisory work with Helen, scrutinising it for my transferential, as well as countertransferential contribution. The parallel process in which I countertransferentially experienced something of what Helen was struggling with in her own work was, with hindsight, readily evident. However, I also puzzled about my excessive efforts to be 'helpful', rather than to stop and explore the difficulty in our working relationship, and came to see that this related to my anxious need to prove my effectiveness to the supervisee who had declared her difficulty in working with men. It then became clear that in my trying too hard, my transference was that I as the 'chosen' man, had to competitively 'prove' myself, where other men had failed. This had been my response to being kept so much in the dark about Helen's feelings about her work.

Before using this material on my work with Helen, I wrote asking her permission. After some time she wrote giving her agreement and also offering some interesting observations which also throw light on her transference to me. I quote:

> I am sorry it has taken me so long to respond. This is about my eighth attempt to (do so . . . I had to) put aside the need to be perfect (and be) handicapped again.

I felt very pleased after our last session that we had been able to communicate and understand each other in a way that hadn't been possible before . . . and walked up the road thinking 'now I could start to have supervision . . . at the same time knowing we'd just finished'. So I was both sad and satisfied.

. . . You are right, I arrived at your door . . . impressed by your reputation and didn't manage to get beyond that until the last session . . . (but I at first felt very angry when I read what you had written).

As I started writing this I suddenly remembered something about my father . . . One day I went to visit him when he was dying of lung cancer and while we were talking he said to me : 'we are strangers' . . . although I knew it was true, I felt gutted . . . The next time I went to visit him, I told him (how upset I had been) and he said 'we two have an affinity' I had an enormous feeling of relief; the connection acknowledged, in place.

Monika

I am seeing Monika, a new supervisee, who is in training, and has approached me for supervision. After a preliminary meeting of the usual sort, we fix a starting date. Then at the first working session, Monika begins to talk non-stop, ostensibly about her patient. After 20 minutes or so, as I am about to say something, Monika talks faster. When I do manage to say something it seems to flow over her. She seems watertight. I find my concentration wandering. I struggle, but nevertheless become dozy, and eventually actually do doze momentarily. We end the session as if nothing untoward has happened. I puzzle over what *has* happened. At the next session, I begin by referring to the previous meeting saying explicitly that I had dozed off and also that I felt concerned about this. Monika says very quickly: 'It's not you. It's me!' I find this statement confusing. We talk a little about her anxiety about coming to me for supervision, and that despite having chosen to come, she fears that my approach to her material might overwhelm her. I also learn that she has a second profession as a performer, and is used to having an appreciative, listening, non-interrupting audience. We both seem relieved to have spoken about the problem and commit ourselves to trying harder and focusing more conscientiously on our task. Also at my suggestion, she undertakes to produce more detailed notes which include both her patients' communications and her inner responses to them.

The next couple of supervisions seem more constructive. Then comes a session in which despite my conscious intentions, I begin to feel increasingly muddled and at a loss, and though I struggle to stay *present* and find some way to engage, my concentration falters and I again become dozy. I find this all the more distressing because the content of what Monika is presenting relates to a difficulty she is having with her patient with which she wants help from me, but I experience her manner as disabling. She speaks in a fast, urgent monotone quoting from her copious notes, and, without seeming to pause for breath, adds more detailed elaborations. I experience the irrational overpowering feeling that if I so much as open my mouth some kind of catastrophe will follow.

During the ensuing week, I begin to seriously wonder whether I will ever be any use to Monika and decide to face this with her at our next meeting. In the event, when we do meet, Monika begins by telling me that she too had been thinking with concern about our last session, and again insists that my dozing off was to do with her. She tells me, as if to reassure me, that although it has not been apparent in the supervision, what has happened between us is proving extremely useful to her in her own therapy. She also mentions that she is currently dealing with some difficult personal problems. As she speaks, there is some mellowing in her tone, and I think that she is beginning to feel less unsafe, and perhaps even a little safe with me. This impression is strengthened as she goes on to say that when she was telling me about her patient the previous week, she was extremely anxious because she knew that the difficulties she was describing as those of her patient were uncomfortably similar to unresolved difficulties of her own relating to her mother. She feared that I would find this out, judge her adversely and report critically on her to her training body.

I say that I am aware that she is putting her trust in telling me all this, and that I think it is also helpful in shedding some light on the difficulties we have both experienced in trying to work together. She says that even though I had not given her my full attention during the session the previous week, and she had noticed when I nodded off, this had been for a brief moment and she had found the supervision session useful and had felt more self contained afterwards; less worried about what she might have to deal with in the next session with her patient. When she says this I realise that my preoccupation about dozing off might have been thus far too tinged with my own sense of guilt for me to try and draw on it as an aspect of the supervisor/supervisee relationship which might be a basis for further self-analytic reflection in the hope of gaining further understanding.

Monika and I do not go any further into what she has said about herself, understanding it as private to her. However, it seems by now clear to me from the way we are conversing with each other that a foundation of trust and co-operation is being established between us. She goes on to volunteer that she had always found it difficult to work with supervisors, and normally copes by trying to intuit what a particular supervisor requires of her, and delivering the goods. She says that she is aware that in performing in this way for supervisors, her own skills are not being supported or developed.

An important factor in our establishing a better level of co-operation was that she enjoyed the support of her training organisation, which though they required supervisors' reports, were relaxed and sophisticated in their understanding of the learning process and supportive of their trainees in a way which did not seek linear evidence of 'progress'. Thus I was able to write a brief honest account of the first 6 months of supervision, agree it with Monika, and have it acknowledged by her training organisation without comment. Reflecting on this process of engagement with Monika, I think we have to some extent changed each other.

I asked Monika if she would consider writing some notes on her experience of our work. I was aware that in asking her to contribute in this way, I was changing the nature of our relationship and did so only after careful thought. On balance I think my suggestion was well received as an invitation for collaborative work, and perhaps even served to consolidate the potential for dialogue in the supervisory relationship. She responded by saying she would think about it, and some weeks later produced her notes. Here is Monika's account:

> The course requires me to have two supervisors to enable me to work with training patients. It was important for me to find supervisors that I would value working with; that I would learn from them. I took trouble to find suitable people – and it was quite a long search. For someone like me in training a supervisor holds a special position between the course, with its distinctive assessments and various pressures, and the personal therapist. Much of the work in therapy concerns personal feelings but the dialogue with the supervisor is very different from the work with the analyst. Because in supervision the two people are able to talk to each other in a much freer way. Both sharing experiences. At first I found it really difficult placing things. Somehow my personal experiences went to my analyst; the patient I brought to the supervisor. But that doesn't work, because in supervision we have to consider my relationship with the supervisor and the patient – linking together forming a triangle.
>
> Initially I felt that I should bring material that would be supervised in the sense of being checked that it was OK and perhaps be told where it was failing. Certainly I had to produce for someone else. It was really hard to take on board that there was someone ready to be of use to me. What I have discovered is that it is for me to bring myself – my feelings, my experiences and share and communicate in such a way that the supervisor is able to tune and be with me, with the patient. What I have found is that it isn't about someone checking on what I have done. Rather that through bringing myself, and sharing my experience, being in attune with another – the supervisor – that through this process it is the work that is to come that is influenced.
>
> I have had an image of the apprentice painters working in a Renaissance

studio. They do the main body of work on a painting. The master adds the finishing touches, details the highlights – bringing a face to life. It seems that the supervisor is able to see – able to reflect from a different perspective; may sometimes give life to experience that might appear routine and dull – and to add subtle tones when the work may become too clever. I think that it is good that there is someone who can challenge – make me reflect on things that might go unnoticed.

Above all it is a triangular unconscious relationship.

It will be apparent that Monika is very clear and imaginative in her writing; and it needs to be said that this stood in some contrast to my ongoing experiences with her (and no doubt also hers with me) in face-to-face dialogue. Despite some important development of co-operation, I was left with a residual sense that there were issues which were still adversely affecting the supervisory work.

Then one morning I woke up from a dream and found myself thinking of Monika with a feeling of sadness. I realised that until then I had consciously felt Monika to be a difficult person to work with, and skirted around the difficulties which we were both having with each other. I realised too that my defensive orientation to Monika had a specific relevance to an aspect of my own early history which had also been a focal point in my own analysis. Recovering this awareness, I approached my task with Monika with a more open state of mind, somehow conveying my deeper sense that the work was difficult for both of us, and this paved the way for a stronger sense of engagement and co-operation between us; with more tolerance of struggle and less pressure to 'achieve'. It became easier for her to share with me how difficult she found the work, especially when it touched on aspects of her own vulnerability, and she began to view me more as someone she could draw on for support, and less as someone to whom she must show how well she was doing.

Sue

The third example is from a supervision session with Sue. This time I offer first my own, then Sue's account of a single supervision session.

Sue tells me that a client who has completed the agreed short-term therapy contract about a year previously, had telephoned requesting urgent help. Sue goes on, and the gist of what she says is:

You remember last time my client was needing help to get out of a relationship in which her partner was doing terrible things to her sexually; and she also worked with her guilt about having watched her sister being buggered as a child . . . Now she is getting some routine support as an outpatient from a community psychiatric nurse, but she says that she can't manage the situation of things being better in her life . . . as if she can't cope without being abused; needs to have that going on. I don't know if she is saying this because of her own insight or because she is being told it in outpatients . . . I don't know why I should have to know . . . What I said to her was that perhaps she was feeling angry with me and with the outpatients – that we had failed her.

As I listen to Sue I notice that she is having difficulty in speaking; her words tumble out and are loosely strung together as if she is unusually anxious and distressed. Registering her style of presentation as well as the impact of the content, I wonder whether the disturbing situation she is describing may be stirring strong personal feelings for her in a way which limits her ability to listen to and think about her client.

I say:

I hear your concern, and you are best placed to understand what your client is communicating, but from what you have said about her here today, it does not sound as if she is expressing anger towards you and the clinic; though it may be that as she has come back for *more* help you have an understandable feeling that you have somehow failed her.

Sue nods.

It may be useful to also consider the possibility that important things may have happened since you and she last met.

Sue replies,

As I am listening to you I am hearing your words as reassuring, but I am having very strong feelings, realising what has been touched for me personally in this situation. It's like suddenly discovering something deeply buried from the past.

I wait. Sue begins to cry. After a short time she says that she has herself been having a difficult time over the last few months. I say:

Perhaps your client has been having a difficult time too in her own way. She may also have some conflicts about what she can tell you. For instance she may feel that she has to justify her return to you in a way which is acceptable, bearing in mind that she came to you originally as a victim of sexual abuse.

I am aware that Sue is wearing a short skirt and sitting in her chair in a way which shows her sleekly stockinged and well shaped legs seemingly drawing my attention to them, and that I find her attractive.

Sue's tears lift, she seems clearer and more energetic. She begins to recall more of her session with her client and talks more freely. She recalls that her client had reported that the community psychiatric nurse had said that the difficulties that were being brought up should be taken back to her previous therapist who was specialised in treating problems relating to sexual abuse. Sue says reflectively that perhaps that was the community nurse's way of passing the buck back because she did not want to deal with the problems which were being brought to her. Sue's whole style of communication seems now much more relaxed: her voice sounds at ease, her sentences are well constructed, and she seems able to think about what she is saying.

I note aloud to Sue that she seems freer to remember and think about her session with her client; as if she has sorted something out. Sue agrees. She now recalls that at the follow-up session, her client had confided that she had experienced the fantasised desire to tear out the genitals of the community nurse. She also reflects on her initial period of work with her client – a year ago – how vivid, detailed and erotically tinged her client's description had been of watching her father engaging sexually with her sister – how Sue herself had felt voyeuristically aroused when her client had described some of these experiences of being a voyeur.

In listening to Sue, I also find myself thinking about the parallel process in which I caught myself registering being attracted by Sue's body. I say

> I wonder whether your client may be burdened by guilt as well as excitement about feeling aroused by seeing her sister being buggered; and her sexual phantasies are again stirred when she looks at the community nurse in Outpatients; you in turn are perhaps invited to, and feel aroused, by her talking about her excitement in watching; and then perhaps a similar atmosphere is evoked here as well; as if all of our erotic fantasies may be being stirred.

Sue responds reflectively:

> Yes, it's everywhere.

I continue,

> Perhaps there is an issue about abuse which still needs further attention, and it is being communicated actively and projectively; and it is important to recognise this and then try and communicate something about your under-standing to your client.

Towards the end of the session, I mention that I am doing some research on the supervisory process, and will be writing up this session and seek her permission before I make any further use of the material. I also ask whether she might consider writing something briefly about her experience of today's supervision session. She said she would think about it. In due course she brought me what she wrote.

Sue's account

I arrive at my supervision after a half-term break. I'm thinking about intending to bring a client who has reapplied after a break of a year. She made an urgent phone call, saying 'I want to see you, Sue.'

I find settling into the supervision session quite difficult. H. has brought me coffee and not one for himself. On the one hand I enjoy being looked after in this way but a single cup emphasises it as not a shared thing.

I need to set the scene; establish the identity of the client. H. remembers her. I refer to the phone message. In the supervision with H. I do not remember the words my client used on the answerphone: 'I want to see you Sue'; so don't report them. I do however emphasise the shock of the new situation, saying that I was taken aback. (As I write these notes now I can see the unconscious significance of my having used the words 'taken aback' when buggery is such a central feature of the case.)

At this point in the supervision I am not able to remember the material from the session I have had with my client . . . I don't know what H. is hearing. I just let myself speak . . . It comes as something of a surprise when I hear what sounds like reassurance from him. He talks about the difficulties of coming back. He asks if I see that as implying failure. He points out that a lot may have happened in a year for me and for my patient. Yes, I think, I've been through some difficult experiences; a love affair that ended suddenly. I'd come back to a supervision after the summer break and been in a tearful state. I know I'm a different person this autumn. In some ways surer but also more vulnerable and less sure. Someone with a new lover. Yes, different; it must change things.

And the client? what has changed for her? But something is changing here, in the supervision session. When I first identify what I hear as reassurance, I feel a flicker of irritation. Surely that's not what I'm asking for? Perhaps I am. As he speaks I begin to apprehend something . . . there's a feeling of something ancient, wordless, deep . . . and echo of something . . . something to do with feeling bad . . . Oh so old. So shitty . . . unacceptable products . . . as if he's speaking to an ancient part of me. I can feel emotion welling up. He sees it. Tears fill me, as they do again as I write this. I put it off, writing it, until now, three weeks after the supervision, drawing on my rough notes. The old fear of criticism, denigration, the old expectations that inhibit presentations in supervision, that feel like exposing vulnerable parts to attack. But, deep down I hear my supervisor saying it's OK. I experience relief. We can acknowledge that something is taking place and that a supervision session is not the place to try and elaborate on it and work it out. Enough that it exists.

Now I begin to recall the session. The obstacle has been removed. The flow can be restored. She has come to tell me she can only cope with life when she is being abused. Her partner, no longer abusing her with his perverse sexual demands, is gone, married to someone else. She said he couldn't cope. She was seeing a woman community psychiatric nurse at the outpatients clinic and told me in a frightened voice that she had fantasies about the woman's healthy genitals, that they were all of a piece with the rest of her. She wanted to attack them, cut them out of her body. By implication, mine too.

H. stops me, he says he has noticed a change in the atmosphere; that I seem to be more freely able to talk about my client now. I agree. H. goes on to say he is writing something up about the process of supervision, and asks whether I might also consider writing a few notes about this session. This sets off a new process in me . . . Could I do it justice? . . .

We go back to my material. She had a sister who she saw being buggered by father and was guilty about the excitement (as well as shock and concern) she had felt. She's aroused by the nurse at the clinic, she arouses a porno-graphic interest in me and I'm telling my male supervisor these things as if (it could be said) I might be arousing him. 'It's all around', I say, getting the sense of the erotic undertows and currents. Who is watching who glimpsing what. The pornographic books under the bed. Our phantasies about each other . . . The couch in the room . . . yes, it's all around. So we are stirred, and like the sugar in the coffee, dissolve to produce a new flavour.

So she returns to me as I return to my supervisor. She came back to the counselling relationship where sexual difficulties might be dealt with.

Now having communicated both Sue's and my notes to you, I find myself wondering whether some of the unconscious processes which may have been transmitted from client to counsellor, to supervisor, may also have been transmitted to you in a way which stirs powerful currents of feeling in you, which may in turn be difficult to contain, and think about. If you do have compelling emotional responses to the material, these may merit exploration and association as a way of further extend-ing the proposition being put forward in this chapter, i.e. that it may be informative for the listener (as well as the supervisor) to address the transferential as well as countertransferential aspect of what is being experienced.

The reader of this chapter can allow time to pause for reflection, free association, day dreaming or even dozing off. There is no responsibility for a supervisee issue. By contrast, my supervisees not infrequently bring to their supervision sessions the stress, headaches, fears, guilt, desire, sleeplessness, nightmares, anger and despair they experience in relation to their patients. At such times the relation to the supervisor in supervision sessions may serve as a source of support, containment, encouragement and affirmation, which clears the space for further effort and discovery, and further learning. Nevertheless the supportive aspect of the supervisory relationship can clearly benefit the supervisee's work; and it is important that it is valued as part of the supervisor's role. In my experience therefore, however much the transferential manifestations in the supervisory relationship are a key to discovery and useful appli-cation, it is also very important that the supervisor is ready to take on a containing role at appropriate times. And indeed at other times to be prepared to risk being a mentor.

On re-reading the above account of the supervision session with Sue and reflecting further on my experience of working with her, I came to the realisation that in my way of relating to her, there was an unconscious element of experiencing her as if she was a favourite talented daughter who flourished with what I was giving her in a way which flattered my narcissism. I then recalled that there had been occasions when I had not attended carefully to material which Sue had brought which might well have illuminated a particular weakness in her approach to her work (as if it was difficult for me to think of her as doing 'wrong'). This realisation led me to think more carefully about certain aspects of her work and opened the way to challenge a particular situation she had described to me. To do so was initially uncomfortable, but in the event was also a relief to her and opened the way to further development.

The group dimension

All three of the above cases are taken from 'dyadic' or rather 'triadic' work, because its clear that in all supervision the 'other' in the form of the client or patient who is the focus of the supervisory work is implicitly present. Besides this triad there are always additional individuals and groupings of individuals present in the mind of both supervisor and supervisee. These may include, at a conscious and/ or unconscious level,

- the peer groups of both supervisor and supervisee
- a training committee
- a supervisee's supervision group
- the supervisor's supervisors
- the supervisee's other supervisor(s)
- both participants' therapists past and/ or present
- the supervisor's supervisors past and present
- books and papers both participants have read
- the professional organisation(s) with which each participant is affiliated
- the cultural and socio-economic matrix in which the work is taking place, and so on
- and of course the whole reticulated tapestry of earliest internalised experiences which manifest themselves as transferences and countertransferences.

To bring the implicit group dimension more out into the open, I will now draw on an example from an actual group supervision session. What follows relates to painful and traumatic events.

I was a visiting facilitator with a single opportunity to work with the group of white South African health professionals some months before the epoch-making 1994 election. The participants were used to drawing on psychoanalytic understanding in relation to their work. After initial mutual introductions and explorations of options, the group decided to begin with a presentation of short-term work by one of those present who consulted to a large organisation. She explained that her role was to be available to members of the work force who were suffering from stress and wanted to consult her. Generally she had a wide range of situations to cope with, but on the particular morning she was telling us about, she had seen two people in one day who had been quite difficult to deal with. The supervisee spoke in an even tone which did not at all prepare me for her account which she narrated in an equally detached sounding voice.

Her first client of the morning had been an African woman who was agitated. After she had had some support in calming down, she began to explain that it was to do with the journey in her shared taxi that morning. She explained that she had missed the bus from the township, and had then had no option but to share the expense of a minibus taxi. The taxi driver had gone along some back roads and they all suddenly found themselves on the edge of a largish group of Africans holding stones as if ready to throw them. Further along the street were a group of uniformed policemen. As the taxi edged forward it became clear that the policemen were pointing their weapons. As the taxi moved closer a shout rang out from one of the policemen: '*Skiet die Kaffirs in die taxi*' ('Shoot the Kaffirs in the taxi'). The taxi driver, hearing this, accelerated for all he was worth, and as the taxi lurched forwards, the sound of bullets rent the air.

The supervisee said she had been able to do little more than listen in the hour available. She added that the woman had seemed less agitated when she left. The supervision group was silent after this account, and before I could encourage further response the presenter said she would also like to talk about her second client, whom she had also seen for just an hour.

The group, who were consulted, clearly supported this, so the supervisee went on. During the same day, a second African woman came for a consultation, seeming in a state of shock. With encouragement she said that her bus had been forced to stop that morning by a group of young men who had blocked off the road. The passengers had then been forced to alight and told that they were required to 'bear witness'. They were led to a piece of waste ground nearby where a man stood bound and blindfolded with a motor tyre round his neck. He was being held by two others. The bus passengers were told that they were required to witness his 'necklacing'. The passengers stood in shocked and frightened silence. The client somehow managed to ask why this man was going to be murdered, and was told roughly that it was because he dealt in witchcraft involving human parts – and a closed box nearby was pointed to. The tyre was then set alight and the passengers forced to watch as he burned to death screaming in agony. The client had begun to shiver as she spoke and then burst into tears. The supervisee had stayed with her a little longer then arranged for someone in the personnel department to find work colleagues to give some support.

I felt absolutely overwhelmed at the end of this account, which was met by a group silence. When I tried to encourage some overt response, there was little forthcoming, only some desultory conversation. Someone said that you could not really do anything in one session, and there seemed a general view that there did not seem any point in doing this kind of work. (I registered but did not comment on the parallels of my only working with the group for a single day.) There was some further unclear conversation . . . and a pressure building to leave this case and move on to considering some long-term work. I more than once drew the group back to the two cases which had been presented, suggesting that perhaps there was more to explore, that perhaps something was being avoided. Then suddenly one member of the group began crying, then weeping, and got up suddenly and rushed from the room screaming, 'I can't bear it'. With my support a friend followed her. In the ensuing atmosphere of shock and uncertainty, one member of the group confronted me challengingly, saying that if I had not led the group in the way that I had, if I had not insisted on staying so long with these issues, we would not now have to cope with all this disturbance. I agreed that that might well be so.

Gradually the group settled and the atmosphere seemed warm and supportive. Then one of the group said to the person who had presented that she very much admired her for her courageous work; she noted that she herself opted for a much less stressful working environment and noted that she and the others speaking today seemed to have given up facing difficult issues. This note was picked up by other group members who, with the exception of the person who had been criticising me, had something positive to say to the presenter. She then began to weep, saying how isolated she felt in her work, and how much she felt alienated from her colleagues and hurt when they had not responded to her earlier.

After a while, the person who had run out returned with her friend. She was still distressed, but apologised to the group and explained that in the last few weeks her own life circumstances had become something of a nightmare. She feared for the future and saw no way out. She also explained that she had given up the kind of work which was being presented today, because she had come to find it too stressful. She had then tried to concentrate on private practice (mainly with whites). The cases presented reminded her of her own distressing experience of similar work, work she had given up and was trying to forget. She was also reminded of her painful feelings of concern for the life situation of a black patient whom she was continuing to see – at a token fee. She felt it was just a gesture which made her feel worse. Certainly psychotherapy, and the practice of being a psychotherapist, seemed to offer no solution to her or her patients, or the country as a whole. Then a whole torrent of feeling was let loose among the remaining members of the group especially relating to the anxiety and tension and pessimism this all-white group was feeling about their future in their country. They spoke about how difficult life was; how pessimistic, frightened and disillusioned they felt. Some had been working collaboratively with African colleagues and friends for change, to develop a multi-racial South Africa; but now they were being dropped, isolated, threatened.

As I listened to and felt for all that was happening and being referred to in the group, I found myself deeply moved and crying. At the same time, one member of the group, referred to earlier, criticised me several times saying that if I had led the group differently we would have had a more constructive experience. I said that although I did not think it was possible to know for certain how the group might have developed if I, or anyone else, had behaved differently, I did also think that I took some responsibility for the way things had gone.

As we approached the end of the session, I said that I wondered whether the fact that I was a stranger who was only with them for one day had also contributed to the difficulty in exploring the case presented and the very strong, almost unbearable, feelings that it had evoked. The presenter replied that she had felt very cautious about bringing her work to this session with me, and had felt she must do so because there was nowhere else to take it. She had experienced me as a detached onlooker and felt quite hostile to me until she had noticed that I too was crying, and then she decided she could trust me. I said that it might be that the people she consulted to had a similar struggle about putting their trust when they had suffered such violent traumas.

I ended the session by inviting each member of the group, if they wanted to, to comment on the session. Several said that they had found the session useful and that they had for the first time in many months been able to bridge the coldness which had become an unspoken feature of their weekly supervision groups. One member said they had learned in action about the 'basic assumption' group processes postulated by Bion (1967), as well as about what constituted a 'work group'. The woman who had been critical maintained her stance, in a tensely defiant tone of voice, stating that my style of leadership had created disturbance, and that with a different leader they could have had a more constructive experience. I noted that in expressing this view now, she seemed to have become quite isolated from the rest of the group, and was concerned that something was being split off on to her (with her collusive involvement). I said that I wanted to acknowledge her courage in sticking to her point of view in criticising me even when she had been alone in doing so. The group seemed surprised at my words. She herself, however, then became a little less tense, and said that although she did not agree with the way I had led the group, she had also been thinking about her own experience over the last few months and realised how disillusioned she had become. She had had a leadership role in a multi-racial, socially-concerned activist group, and at their last election she had not even been elected on to the committee. She realised she had become bitter and felt dumped. She also thanked me and the group for allowing her to express her critical views; and not shutting her up. The group ended on that note.

Some considerable time later I consulted a member of the group about the above notes, asking for his views specifically about whether confidentiality had been protected and the extent to which my account accorded with his memory of the experience. He responded in due course, in writing, stating that though he thought confidentiality was generally well protected (with one exception which I have since modified), what my notes missed was the 'sense of time'. I quote:

> I think you have captured the day very well indeed, and I was quite moved reading it through. One point I would suggest you add is something about the sense of time which I do think you miss. In your account, things happen too quickly, and miss the sense of how the group ineptly struggled with the material presented. I still think we tried to respond as we thought therapists should – without losing distance and dignity. I think we all struggled with what response was permitted within the group; with emotion not being really allowed. Be that as it may, 'some desultory conversation' . . . does not quite capture the extended silences; the pained awkwardnesses; no one seeming to quite know what to say; the slow dawning awareness of the inadequacy of our response to the presenter and her material; and so on. I would just add in a word or two around these things. Certainly, I agree that one component of all this was a mounting pressure to get away from the political and personal immediacy of the presented material, and get onto some nice safe long term work that one could view through a long psychodynamic lens. You might even say something about how you quite explicitly said that if we wanted to know what a defended group was, we were a good example (an indication of how hard we worked to keep away from the issues in the room and of how hard you had to work to get us back to them).

With the help of these comments I came to realise on further reflection, something of my ambivalent transference to the group, recognising evidence of my own unconscious negative feelings in 'forgetting' how difficult a struggle the group had had; and also that I had somewhat aggressively spelled out (as if we did not all see it), that 'they' were a 'defended' group. At a deeper level, they represented to me a family –

that aspect of my family – (and motherland), which I myself had left behind because I had not been able to bear to stay, and towards whom I therefore felt guilty. Thus my feelings of concern, and countertransference awareness that something was being denied by the group, was operating alongside my transference which included my own angry defensiveness to cover my unconscious feelings of guilt.

Further reflections

In supervision, unlike in therapy, participants are brought together in the interests of the supervisee's absent patient. The supervisee, if still in training, will frequently have the benefit of an ongoing own therapy or analysis, which is a constant reminder of the ubiquity of the transference. By contrast, the supervisor has less current support for, and may be less likely to be open to, registering the working of unconscious transferences emanating from the supervisor and projected on to the supervisee.

Bion (1967) remarked that in psychoanalysis 'the transference is to the total situation'. To endeavour to extend this way of thinking to supervision in those contexts when a supervisee is 'in training', we need to be mindful that the 'total situation' in supervision always includes two different internal representations of the training committee. This is highlighted when the supervisor provides the training committees with reports. I have found that the loaded power dynamics introduced can be mitigated if the supervisor reports first to the supervisee, and then takes account of the supervisee's response in producing a final report, of which the supervisee is given a copy. This may reduce feelings of infantilisation in the trainee and contributes to increased trust, especially if the supervisor then also encourages the supervisee to review and assess the supervisor's performance.

I now turn, briefly, to the supervision of training therapists who are coming for supervision in relation to their work as therapists of trainees. First of all, it is obviously necessary for this supervisor to be an outsider who does not know the trainee. Even so, as supervisor, I have learned to become aware of, and deal with, my positive identification with the training therapist which can risk pulling me off task. For example, on one occasion, a supervised training therapist in presenting his work with a particular trainee conveyed in passing that his patient was having a tough time with the training committee. I first passed this by as 'fact'. then realised that I was also automatically taking the training therapist's view of his colleague's functioning. When I explored this further internally it became clear that my positive transference to the therapist contained split-off negative feelings towards the training committee. It was then possible to take up aspects of the therapist–trainee–training committee dynamic with my supervisee in a way which enabled him to 'unhook' himself from identifying with the projective aspect of his trainee patient's experience of the training committee. The patient was then able to integrate his split-off negative feelings and move on to connect with painful, yet integrative, ambivalence in relation to the therapist. (I hope this rather tortuous account is clear!)

This propensity to splitting off the negative, I think, also pervades so much of our profession. Indeed the history of analytical psychology and psychoanalysis and the therapies derived and developed from them, is, on the shadow side, littered by projections, including both idealisation and denigration by, of contributors to our pool of knowledge. Even those who have themselves made important original contributions are sometimes less than even-handed in their critique of those with apparently competing or contradictory views (transference at work again?). As no one can conceivably be 'completely' analysed; if we view unconscious processes as inherently unconscious and only open to active discovery and re-discovery – to be worked again and again rather than conquered – then the value is in learning the method, not in enshrining the 'truth' even about oneself. We can only continue with conviction that the analytic approach continues to reveal ongoing aspects unconscious at work.

Thus as supervisor I need to receive all that is said on trust, but also to be open to standing back and attentive to discovering new meanings which are relevant to my task: I need to be 'open to all possibilities' (Gardner, in press). In supervision, as in therapy, there is never a reliable substitute for ongoing work with the 'here and now' including the supervisor's openness to his or her own projections of the moment, whether these are depressive or paranoid, or archetypal.

To conclude, the view of supervision which I find most useful is that it is primarily a relationship between those present in which the primary task (to support, encourage and inform the work with the absent other[s]) is best fostered by drawing on the supervisor's direct experience in the supervisory dyad or group. Supervision, like therapy, requires active evenly suspended attention to all internal as well as external stimuli; including, that is, the supervisor's transference to the supervisee. The absent patient and all the other significant people and groupings who may appear in supervision, can both be respected as 'real' in their own right; *and* reflected as related to the unconscious dynamics of the supervisory relationship.

The boundaries between supervision and therapy can and must be clearly drawn in terms of the different aims, objectives and methods of the two tasks. However, the underlying way of listening and gathering understanding and being open to insight is the same for the therapist and supervisor. Just as, as therapists, we remain mindful of the illusion that we 'know' the people our patients keep telling us about, so, as supervisors, we need especially to monitor our assumptions about 'knowing' our supervisees' patients.

Supervisors 'can supervise boringly or joyfully' (Sharpe, 1995b). It is important therefore that the methods used hold the supervisor's interest, as well as being supportive to the supervisee.

I am grateful to those of my supervisees who worked with me both in supervision and the research. I think we all learned something and I know my approach to supervision changed in the process.

References and further reading

Bion, W. (1967) *Second Thoughts*. London: Heinemann.

Brett, E. and Hahn, H.(1961) Prejudice – a study on a world theme. *Race Relations Journal* (South Africa) 28(4): 15–21.

Crick, P. (1992) Good supervision: on the experience of being supervised. *Psychoanalytic Psychotherapy* 5(3): 235–45.

Gardner, F. (in press) Open to all possibilities. *British Journal of Psychotherapy*.

Hahn, H. (1985) Transference and countertransference in practice. *British Journal of Psychotherapy* 21(1): 20–9.

Hahn, H. (1988) On establishing the psychotherapeutic alliance in an unsophisticated environment. *British Journal of Psychotherapy* 4: 30.

Hess, A.L. (ed.) (1980) *Psychotherapy Supervision*. New York: Wiley.

Klein, M. (1952) Notes on schizoid mechanisms in developments in psycho-analysis. *International Psycho-analytic Library* 43. London: Hogarth Press.

Oberman, C. (1990) In *Supervision and the Achievement of an Analytic Identity* (ed. Robert C. Lowe). New York: Brunner/Mazel.

Rayner, E. and Hahn, H.(1964) Assessment for psychotherapy. *British Journal of Medical Psychology* 37: 331–42.

Sharpe, M. (ed.) (1995a) *The Third Eye: Supervision of Analytic Groups*. London: Routledge.

Sharpe, M. (1995b) Participating in groups effectively, Chapter 4 in *The Third Eye: Supervision of Analytic Groups* (ed. M. Sharpe). London: Routledge.

Smith, B. (1994) The supervisory process. In *Proceedings of the Severnside Institute for Psychotherapy Study Weekend*. Bristol: Severnside Institute Publications.

Stimmel, B. (1995) Resistance to awareness of the supervisors transferences with special reference to the parallel process. *International Journal of Psycho-Analysis* 76: 609–18.

Symington, N. (1993) *Narcissism. A New Theory*. London: Karnac.

Tsegos, Y.T. (1995) A Greek model of supervision. In *The Third Eye: Supervision of Analytic Groups* (ed. M. Sharpe) pp. 116–30. London: Routledge.

Chapter 7
Supervision in bereavement counselling

SUSAN LENDRUM AND GABRIELLE SYME

Functions of supervision

The word 'supervision' in counselling refers to a relationship between a counsellor and another, usually more experienced counsellor, who ideally has some further training in counselling supervision. It is sometimes called 'consultative support' in order to avoid confusion with other meanings of 'supervisor', which entail ideas of 'inspector' or 'overseer', with the corresponding suggestions of incompetence or formal assessment. Practising counsellors meet regularly, either individually or in small groups (3–4 people), with their supervisors or with peer groups to talk through and reflect upon their counselling sessions. The choice of individual, small group or peer group supervision might be simply pragmatic, and based on availability. However, it is important to recognise that peer group supervision is only suitable for experienced counsellors, and even then it should not be the only supervision. A fairly typical duration and frequency for individual supervision would be 1 hour every fortnight, and for peer and small group supervision 1½ hours every fortnight.

In Lendrum and Syme (1992) we have tried to give some idea of how the counselling attitudes, sensitivity and knowledge might look when translated into 'skills'. We also likened the integration of counselling skills into the counselling relationship, to the integration of skills required in the co-ordination necessary to ride a bicycle. But of course the counselling relationship is more than that; it is a living interchange between two human beings, who are both experiencing and learning within that relationship. One of the ways in which the counsellor learns from, and about, the counselling relationship and about how to develop it more effectively, is through this confidential supervision relationship.

In supervision a counsellor is able to focus on the interaction with the client in a collaborative and supportive environment. The supervisor recognises and works with the feelings experienced in the counselling session, as well as those experienced in the supervisory session.

Such a 'place for feelings' is very necessary, for in choosing to enter the world of other people's losses counsellors are entering something different from the normal and the everyday. There are times when it may seem barely worthwhile to the counsellor. Clients can be consistently ungrateful, can get stuck in suicidal feelings and do, albeit occasionally, succeed in committing suicide. Counsellors can think they have lost their way and feel useless, helpless and drained. It would hardly be surprising, then, that counsellors can come to believe they have nothing more to give, or have been a failure. At times like this it is tempting to 'soldier on', to 'keep the head down', to 'get on with it' and not make time to reflect in supervision on what is going on in the counselling relationship. Individuals, teams and organisations can all collude in this process of 'head down', 'soldier on' and denial of the necessity for supervision. This denial may occur out of the mistaken, but common, belief that remembering and reflecting on pain 'only makes it worse'. Yet it is this very reflecting and sharing, in the context of a secure and professional supervisory relationship, which can offer comfort and care for the counsellor's struggle with the client. Supervision can also offer a place to reflect upon the skills and interventions which are being used as well as those which are being avoided. It can then enable the counsellor to ponder the reasons for avoidance of certain skills or feelings; or to wonder why certain rules of counselling practice are suddenly particularly difficult to follow.

A loss counsellor then can expect supervision to function in three ways:

- As a safe and secure base in which to feel, and to reflect upon feelings, images and associations which arise. This is sometimes called the *restorative function*.
- As a place to develop appropriate skills and abilities through reflecting upon and learning from the nitty-gritty of the relationship. This is sometimes called the *formative function*.
- As a place to reflect as honestly and openly as possible about the quality of the counselling work and its relationship to professional standards and codes of practice. This is sometimes called the *normative function*.

These 'restorative, formative and normative functions of supervision' (Proctor, 1988), although theoretically possible to describe as if they were discrete and separate entities, are in practice seldom totally separate.

We shall start by describing each function in turn and then give a brief illustration of how they interweave.

The restorative function

For an inexperienced counsellor a sense of security will be enhanced through training. This fosters self-awareness and acceptance, and confirms and develops skills. None the less even for the most experienced counsellor the very strong feelings associated with the void, emptiness, suicidal despair and essential loneliness of human existence, can emerge in the process of grieving and evoke fear and insecurity. The counsellor who wishes to remain receptive to this experience in others, needs to be allowed to feel such emotional disturbance within the safer setting of the supervisory relationship. To create a safe environment for this type of exploration the supervisor needs to demonstrate the attitudes of empathy, warmth and genuineness, and hence create an accepting environment. In such a climate the counsellor can feel secure enough to explore, ponder and reflect upon the counsellor–client relationship in a way which ensures and develops the effectiveness of that relationship. We can draw a parallel here between supervision and John Bowlby's work on attachment.

The work of Bowlby (1969) showed that parents who are secure within themselves, and who are not over-anxious about themselves or their world, offer their children a secure base from which to explore. This, in turn, leads to the children feeling secure enough to be able to explore, enjoy and understand the world. Of course, children will get hurt and frightened in the course of their explorations, but they will return to the secure base for comfort and healing before setting out again. In a similar way the supervisor, who is personally secure, offers a 'secure base' where the counsellor can return for comfort and healing. The counsellor is then in a better position to 'set out' and offer a secure and predictable relationship to a client. This will be very necessary for a client who is hurt, frightened and in need of security in a world which has become chaotic and unpredictable through loss.

To offer such a secure base the supervisors too must keep confronting and experiencing these deeply human issues with their own supervisors or consultants. A further way in which the security of supervision is enhanced is through a clear contract. This needs to be negotiated along the lines of the 'Code of Practice' section of the British Association for Counselling's (BAC) Code of Ethics and Practice for Supervisors of Counsellors.

Obviously the restorative function of supervision has similarities to personal counselling, but only in as far as the environment of acceptance is essential to create trust. Beyond that the focus is entirely different. In supervision the primary focus is the counsellor's client; in personal counselling the focus would be on the counsellor.

The formative function

For an inexperienced counsellor supervision often focuses on the task of relating theoretical ideas to the actual practice of counselling. There is likely therefore to be a substantial training aspect to supervision in the early stages. The counsellor will also be helped to look very closely at which skills were used in the session and which were not. Further areas of exploration would be to look at the consequences of these interventions, and to help counsellors become more aware of their responses, and sometimes reactions, to the client and in return to consider the client's reactions. As the counsellor gains experience, supervision focuses more and more on understanding what is going on in the relationship. We sometimes use the word 'process' for this 'what-is-going-on-in-the-relationship'. Reflecting upon this process of the counselling relationship and trying to understand the particular pattern of grief constitutes the 'meat', as it were, of supervision. Other less conscious processes relating to supervision will be considered later in this chapter.

The normative function

Supervisors within almost any context will have some responsibility to ensure that the counsellor's work is appropriate and falls within defined ethical standards. Given that the primary purpose of supervision is to ensure that the counsellor is addressing the needs of the client, the supervisor will be concerned with ethical issues of counselling. This includes concern about confidentiality, respect for the client's beliefs and values, and maintenance of the boundaries between counselling and friendship. The supervisor also needs to recognise whether the counsellor is too depleted by the work to continue counselling; or too affected by the losses brought to the work to continue without having either a break from counselling, further training, personal counselling or even all three. The supervisor's task within this function is to monitor the overall quality of the work. The BAC publishes Codes of Ethics and Practice for counsellors and for those using Counselling Skills, in addition to the one for supervisors mentioned earlier.

The interweaving of supervisory functions

To show how these various supervisory functions interweave in the supervision of loss counselling we shall look at Angie's story.

Angie's story

Angie was able to pick up the threads of her life again after her lover Oliver's death: not without great pain and sorrow, but with increased sensitivity and a new maturity. After that there followed a period of enormous personal and professional development for Angie. Gradually she was able to invest her renewed energy into her work and grow in confidence and personal strength. About 3½ years after Oliver's death Angie met Paul, who himself was suffering loss. His ex-wife Sally, from whom he had separated 4 years previously, but who had continued to live down the road, had decided to move to northern Scotland taking his 4-year-old daughter Katie. Angie not only 'knew' about loss in the historical sense of having experienced loss herself, she also 'knew' about loss in the sense of knowing that the feelings of grief need to be heard and understood. She knew that it would take time for ambivalent feelings to be disentangled and resolved and that the process cannot be rushed. Therefore she was not only able to wait for Paul to grieve the profound loss of Sally and Katie, but was also able to help him in his grief. Knowing that Paul's loving feelings towards Sally and Katie did not prevent loving feelings growing in their own relationship, Angie was able to tell Paul a great deal about Oliver. This allowed Angie to treasure the precious memories of the man who had died so young. Angie and Paul's relationship developed through their separate griefs, they were married two years later and went on to have two children of their own.

Over the years, as the children became more independent, Angie realised that she was interested in going forward for selection as a bereavement counsellor. In thinking about the selection process, she wondered whether the wound of Oliver's death 10 years earlier had healed enough for her to be in a position to offer herself for counselling training. She thought that it had.

Angie was indeed selected as a counsellor, took part in initial training and began working with her first clients. She had group supervision at the training centre and saw her individual supervisor once a fortnight.

One day a new client, Debbie, came in to see Angie and quickly burst into tears. The following is the story she had to tell.

Debbie's story

Debbie was a student and had recently gone to university. The day before she had left home for university she had received a letter out of the blue from her boyfriend, John, her first love, saying quite coldly that the relationship was finished. He was going to college, she to university, and their ways ought to part. Debbie had been distraught at this news and had sought comfort from her mother, but her mother seemed to reject her feelings and kept insisting that 'there were other fish in the sea'. This made Debbie feel even worse and it was at that point that she had sought counselling at the agency where Angie worked.

Two days after this initial session Angie was able to take the work to her supervisor, David. The following story illustrates the restorative, formative and normative functions of supervision.

The first memory Angie had was that Debbie had been very distressed, and that she was grieving the loss of her young man, John, at much the same age she had been when Oliver died. She then remembered that she had wondered momentarily whether she should refer Debbie to someone else. However, she had felt secure enough in herself to leave the idea of referral and get on with the work with Debbie in the session. In supervision she wanted to review this decision, and to consider further whether the empathic skills she had used had been appropriate and effective. As Angie talked with her supervisor, David, about her initial assessment she realised that she had noticed three crucial factors which had suggested to her the appropriateness of a counselling relationship for Debbie. First Debbie had talked of student friends in a way that made Angie think she was well supported. Second Angie noticed Debbie's open distress and anger, which seemed to indicate that the grief-work was under way. Finally Angie had sensed a growing trust and developing relationship as the counselling session progressed. Angie herself felt well supported in the supervisory relationship so she realised, encouraged by her supervisor, that she should continue with Debbie rather than refer.

As the supervision session proceeded Angie remembered Debbie's anger, and also began to remember, with poignant intensity, how angry she herself had felt when she had experienced feelings of abandonment by Oliver. Gradually as she talked about those feelings of loss, abandonment, and anger, she became aware that Debbie's anger was different from her own. However, she realised that she had the capacity to understand and empathise with Debbie. She realised, with David's help, that she had grieved Oliver enough to be able to work with Debbie on Debbie's grief. This enabled her to focus on the feelings in relation to Debbie which she was still aware of from the session. She could remember the interventions she had used, and reflect on what their effect might have been on the counselling relationship. She could then consider alternative interventions and think with her supervisor about how she might have ended the session more effectively. This led on to a brief discussion about the particular importance of firm boundaries in loss counselling.

In the supervision session described above we have shown how the three main functions of supervision interweave. At the beginning of the session, supervision is mainly formative, as Angie reflects on the relationship with Debbie. In reflecting on her feelings of anger the function of the supervision moves into the restorative mode; and then back into the formative mode, as Angie returns the focus to understanding Debbie and working with Debbie's anger. There are further examples of the movement from formative to reflective and back again before the final part of the supervision, which is normative.

Uses of feelings

The counsellor's feelings

In the above description of a supervisory session we have focused on the various feelings which are evoked in the counsellor and which are a particularly important part of supervision. First of all this focusing helps the counsellor to discover whether these feelings belong more to the client or more to the counsellor. If they belong to the counsellor it is important to establish whether they can be contained within the supervisory session, and then used to understand more about the client; or whether they signal the need for personal counselling for the counsellor. This focus on the feelings is both restorative, in that it helps contain the feelings naturally evoked by working with loss, and formative in that the discovery may be made that certain feelings, experienced by the sensitive counsellor, may well be the very feelings denied by the client. Awareness of the existence and nature of all these feelings is an important part of the counsellor's development.

We shall now return to Angie to look in more detail at how the supervisor helps the counsellor use her feelings remembered from the counselling session. In her supervision session with David we see how Angie's feelings were contained and then used to give a clue to Debbie's difficulties.

Use of counsellor's feelings to locate denied feelings in the client

In the supervision session described above Angie found that her feelings about Oliver, re-awakened by the counselling work, could be heard and contained within the supervision session. She was then able to focus back on to her session with Debbie. As she did this she became aware of an intensely sad and aching feeling in herself, which she had first felt as she listened to Debbie raging about this 'awful' John. Debbie seemed still to be protecting herself from feelings of pain and sadness by raging at and vilifying John. Angie seemed to sense the feelings, which Debbie dared not. David, her supervisor, in pondering about these feelings with her, helped her to see that not only the anger but also the feelings of sadness and pain belonged to Debbie. They then discussed ways in which Angie might reflect back the anger and rage which Debbie was expressing, and hint at the sadness and longing of which Debbie seemed unaware. This would give Debbie an opportunity, within the context of the counselling relationship, to experience the feelings of which she was afraid.

Use of counsellor's feelings to recognise the counsellor's need

When the feelings stirred up in a counsellor by a particular client keep distracting the counsellor from the counselling relationship, they may be signalling to the counsellor that certain ungrieved losses in her own life need attention. The following account is given by a counsellor who experienced powerful feelings in the counselling session, which later in supervision she recognised as her own.

'About 10 years ago now I remember how, towards the end of a counselling session with Jenny, I felt my throat tighten and tears coming to my eyes. Jenny was grieving the loss, through abortion, of the only child she might have had with the man who had just left her.

Of course I might well have shed tears for Jenny in her hitherto unrecognised grief, but my tears here were strangely distracting and I felt uncomfortable and angry in the session. A few days later in my supervision session I was able, in a safe place, to ponder these feelings and discovered great pain and sadness about a miscarriage I had had some 16 years previously. The relationship with the baby's father had also been lost. It became clear that personal material related not just to the miscarriage, but to the relationship itself, had been re-stimulated in me by Jenny's experiences. The exploration of Jenny's experiences had uncovered more grief in me than could be appropriately dealt with in supervision. I felt considerable relief when my supervisor suggested that I should do some further counselling work in order to explore and work through the feelings from my own grief.

On realising that these distractions came from a past experience of mine, I understood what had interfered with my listening to Jenny. After the supervision session I was able to get help with my own grief. When I met Jenny again the following week I was able 'to be' with her more fully, undistracted by feelings which belonged to my past'.

This example illustrates how the supervisor had helped this counsellor to express and understand some of her feelings about her own miscarriage, and lost relationship. The counsellor quickly recognised her own need to get help with her grief. This then enabled the counsellor to empathise with Jenny's conscious feelings, as well as focusing on her feelings at the edge of awareness. She was now responding to Jenny the person, rather than simply reacting to material which Jenny had brought.

Not all feelings felt in a session are necessarily distracting. In supervision we will recall many feelings as we remember a session. One example might be that we felt deskilled. Supervision could help us understand whether the deskilled feeling related quite straightforwardly to poor use of skills; or whether feelings of deep insecurity, or hopelessness in the client were being experienced by the counsellor, as if they were her own. Obviously many other feelings felt by the counsellor, when recalling a counselling session in supervision, can be used in this way to understand what is happening in the relationship.

In the previous example with Jenny, a source of learning for the counsellor occurred when feelings, expressed by the griever during the session, immediately re-evoked forgotten and unresolved feelings that had gone underground in the counsellor long ago. In supervision she was quickly aware of the feelings and their source and acknowledged what needed to be done. It sometimes happens, however, that feelings or processes from the client do not reach the counsellor's conscious awareness and so she brings them or 'reflects' them unconsciously into the supervision relationship.

Reflected feelings in the parallel process

This phenomenon of unconscious material from the counselling relationship finding its way into the supervisory relationship was first pointed out by Harold Searles (1955). He described how the processes in the one relationship are repeated or reflected in the processes in the other relationship. This is the basis for what is called the parallel process which happens frequently in supervision.

When the counsellor unconsciously parallels the client's behaviour in supervision it can throw light on the counselling relationship. This happened to one of us recently when counselling Christopher.

Christopher talked of his lover Jake who had recently died of AIDS. He was angry, isolated and very frightened of trusting me. He came into the first session more or less shouting, 'Just how do you think you can help me? Do you know what it feels like to have your lover die? You can't give him back to me can you?' I had responded with something like, 'Christopher, you are really angry. Your anger certainly makes sense when you have been so let down. I guess you might be really wary about trusting me in case I let you down too?' I felt reasonably sure that this response was appropriate yet Christopher replied with a 'Yes, but why should I trust you anyway?' And so the session continued with Christopher apparently unable to hear, to take in or to use anything I said. By the end of the session I felt pretty useless.

I took this case to supervision hoping, or so I thought, to get some help with this 'difficult' client, but found myself exceedingly resistant to what I usually regarded as excellent supervision. My responses of 'Yes, but . . .' soon reached my supervisor's awareness and she was able to point out how the process of 'yes-but-resistance' from the counselling session was being reflected in supervision. Once I had become aware of how I was resisting in supervision I realised that this process of resistance was unnecessary there. I could then reflect with my supervisor on how I might work with, and constructively use, Christopher's process of resistance, rather than just be dragged down and made impotent by it.

Use of the supervisor's feelings

There is another way in which unconscious material from the counselling session finds its way into the supervisory session. A supervisor
may pick up an unconscious feeling, which can arise quite suddenly. In
paying attention to this 'stray' feeling the supervisor can often provide
reflective illumination for the counsellor. Angie's supervisor, David,
picked up just such a strong feeling during the first supervision session
soon after Angie had seen her new client Debbie.

You will remember how Debbie had sought comfort from her mother
who had ignored Debbie's feelings, insisting that 'There were other fish
in the sea'. It was at this point that Debbie had sought counselling.
Angie subsequently told David about her session with Debbie. In the
following passage David describes part of this supervisory session with
Angie.

*'I was listening to Angie talking about Debbie's sudden loss and
something to do with Debbie's mother, when I noticed Angie's curious
blankness. Then I found that I wasn't really listening to Angie any more
and was feeling inexplicably angry. I quickly reflected on whether I
might be feeling angry about anything in my own life outside the
session. I thought not. I returned to Angie, pretty certain that this feeling
in me was something to do with Angie and possibly also with her relationship with Debbie. I stopped Angie's talk with some difficulty and
invited her to reflect on whether this inexplicable angry feeling which I
was experiencing could have anything to do with the counselling relationship between her and Debbie. Angie reflected on this. She gradually
became aware that she too had been unable to concentrate fully on
Debbie, when Debbie was talking about her mother.*

*As Angie reflected on her own blankness about Debbie and her
mother she found herself beginning to feel angry. At this point I had
wondered if this was Debbie's anger, which Angie was beginning to feel
(see page 100), but she seemed to draw away from Debbie and towards
her own past. She then suddenly remembered telling her own mother
of Oliver's diagnosis. Her mother, no doubt trying to be helpful at the
time, and perhaps not realising the depth of the relationship between
Angie and Oliver, had said something like "Never mind dear, there are
other pebbles on the beach". Angie also remembered that she had been
so shocked and numbed by the news of Oliver at that point, that she
had felt relatively little about her mother's response.*

*She had subsequently been enabled through counselling to express
her feelings of grief about Oliver's death and now, in supervision,
reflected briefly upon that experience. Her sense was that the 'wound'
had largely healed. It was then that she began to experience and to
express anger about her own mother's response. This was anger which
she had not been able to feel at the time of Oliver's death and which*

*had gone underground. Having been unable to experience or express her own anger with her mother then, Angie had been unable later to recognise that Debbie was angry with **her** mother now.*

I then understood why Angie had been unable to experience her angry feelings in the session with Debbie. I also understood why she had needed to bring them unconsciously, masked by her blankness, into the supervision session. Once Angie had expressed anger about her own mother's similar remarks, she found that she was still angry. This at last was Debbie's anger which had been denied in the counselling session. We were then able to focus on the related counselling tasks. She could then see that Debbie might be needing to recognise, understand and accept her anger with her mother, rather than just her anger with John for leaving her.

These examples show two ways in which unconscious material appears in the supervision session. Others occur whenever processes which happen in the counselling session are, often without the counsellor's awareness, reflected or 'paralleled' in supervision. The supervisor's awareness of these processes is an enormously useful contribution to the understanding of the counselling relationship.

In this chapter we have considered the three main functions of supervision and tried to show how these interrelate in practice. We have also tried to show how both the counsellor's and the supervisor's feelings constitute a rich and necessary resource for understanding the counselling process. What has been implied throughout this chapter, but perhaps needs stating more explicitly, is that it is the quality of the relationship between the counsellor and the supervisor which is paramount. It is when both counsellor and supervisor can drop their judgemental attitudes, face the anxieties inherent for both in the supervisory relationship and manage to be genuine with each other, that the supervision is likely to be most effective.

We have talked here of the necessity of supervision for all counsellors, and of the special quality of supervision for all those working with loss and grief. The importance of supervision is highlighted by BAC in its schemes for the accreditation of both counsellors and supervisors. Counsellors are required to show a commitment to ongoing supervision and continuing personal development through training.

Supervision itself has training-like qualities in its formative function, but cannot replace a training course in counselling skills or counselling. Any more advanced training course in counselling will include either group or individual supervision as part of the course.

Summary

Supervision is a relationship between either one or several loss counsellors and a more experienced counsellor (working as a supervisor).

The primary focus is the well-being of the clients, with the care and development of the counsellors as a very close secondary focus.

Care for the counsellor is paramount in the lonely business of loss counselling, where the pain of grief is a consistent element of the work. The tendency in our culture to deny pain can lead to a similar tendency to deny the need for supervision.

Supervision functions in three main ways:

- as a restorative base where the feelings stirred up by grief work may be expressed, contained and reflected upon
- as a formative or developmental forum for studying the theoretical implications, the interventions and the processes of the counselling relationship.
- as a place for monitoring the quality of counselling through such normative elements as maintaining appropriate boundaries, adhering to codes of ethics and practice, etc.

Sometimes supervisory activities fulfil more than one function simultaneously, and at other times supervision moves almost imperceptibly from one function to another.

Some feelings and processes which are not conscious in the counselling relationship may be brought unconsciously into the supervisory relationship. The supervisor's awareness and use of this material is an integral part of supervision.

References

Bowlby, J. (1969) *Attachment and Loss: 1 – Attachment.* London: Hogarth Press.

Lendrum, S. and Syme, G. (1992) *Gift of Tears*, Chapters 9, 10 and 13. London: Routledge.

Proctor, B. (1988) *Supervision: A Working Alliance,* (videotape training manual). St. Leonards-on-Sea: Alexia.

Searles, H. (1955) The informational value of the supervisor's emotional experiences. *Psychiatry* 18: 135–146.

Chapter 8
The ethical dimensions of supervision

LESLEY MURDIN AND PETRŪSKA CLARKSON

Theory and practice

Supervision as an ethical enterprise for carers is, we know, a multi-dimensional enterprise which requires both the exercise of considerable skill and also an awareness of the part played by ethics and values in all that we do. Psychotherapy has so far resisted attempts to see it and practise it as a science with a body of tested theory and a range of techniques agreed and practised by all. The Strasbourg Declaration of the European Association for Psychotherapy declares that psychotherapy is a scientific discipline governed by scientific method. We all position ourselves somewhere along the spectrum that leads from replicability and generalisable truths at one end to the art of responding to the individual and his or her unique self at the other end. Nevertheless, to ignore research findings from psychology, physics and mathematics seems to blindfold us unnecessarily; on the other hand, not to spend time considering the part played by the values on which a therapist and supervisor might be basing their work would be equally disabling.

Supervision has its laws. The British Association for Counselling (BAC) was the first organisation to have written a code of ethics and practice for supervisors (BAC, 1995), although the British Association for Psychoanalytic and Psychodynamic Supervision (BAPPS) has since produced its own code as well. These codes set out guidelines and requirements for attitudes and conduct in the practice of supervision. These work well for the majority of supervisory relationships most of the time, but sooner or later everyone comes across a conflict or an ambivalence where the code is not sufficient guidance.

Because the spirit of the law is as important as the letter of the law, we also need to consider the values that underlie the work of the supervisor (Clarkson and Murdin, 1996). Since the work of psychotherapy supervision is in relationship and about relationship, any discussion of the ethical questions facing supervisors will have to take into account the complexities of all the relationships involved in supervision. We are always working in supervision with a role that may range between levels of responsibility depending on whether the work is with a trainee or an experienced colleague. The supervisor shifts into a different register but the exact positioning of a given piece of work may need careful thought.

There are legal and ethical considerations as well as the more personal ones of taste and inclination and, very importantly, the model of work being supervised, which will inevitably affect the values underlying the supervision. For example, at its most obvious, the importance of working with countertransference may vary depending on the extent to which the model emphasises intra-psychic as distinct from inter-psychic processes. We may think of these aspects of the work in metaphorical terms as the depth at which it is carried out. In addition to the dimension of depth, we are also bound to be concerned with the topographical dimensions of the relationships involved.

A map of supervision

Supervision involves an extremely complex interacting system. Figure 8.1 shows the basic subsystems present in any supervision. They all have their own values attached and their own ethical, moral and legal compulsions both conscious and unconscious. This map provides a way of diagrammatically locating where the supervisor may most fruitfully focus attention. The discussion which follows takes the supervisor's vantage point.

The supervisor's relationship with the supervisee's client

The supervisor's primary concern should be with the welfare of the client. Our concern in this chapter is to look at the conflicts that might be implied by the supervisor's concern for the client having to meet the concern for and the actual contract with the supervisee.

Consider the following dilemma. A therapist, Mrs P, is seeing a very angry client, Mrs C. The client makes great demands on the therapist. She has suffered a great many losses in that both her parents died when she was small and she was brought up by a succession of aunts who passed her from one to another like a parcel. She now has two children of her own, aged three and five, and no partner present. She is tempted to hit the children and has been coming to counselling for several months in order to try to understand this violence in herself.

The therapist finds this whole subject difficult to work with and has just decided to go on a two week holiday because she is over-tired. You

Figure 8.1. Overlapping supervisory systems (This is a version of a diagram first published in Clarkson, 1997.)

(the supervisor) know that she is tired but you also suspect that the therapist is not dealing well with the resonances that this client's situation has with her own background. You may well have no choice in this matter over what is done, but you do have a choice over whether to say anything, and how much you say.

The supervisor's relationship with the supervisee's psychotherapist

Another relationship which gives rise to possible ethical and technical difficulties is the relationship, often unacknowledged, of the supervisor with the supervisee's psychotherapist. This is a relationship that is potentially fraught with conflict or collusion. The conclusions that the supervisor draws about the therapist are bound to be deductions from the supervisee's behaviour and responses, and will tend to come to mind when there are problems. The thought that arises is that this blind spot should have been picked up by the therapist. Questions about the psychotherapist's competence, motivation or insight may arise.

In the case of Mrs P, the supervisor might well hope that the therapist would know what was happening and would be working with the source of avoidance. This is a reasonable hope, but Mrs P. is likely to be avoiding in her own therapy as well as in her work. The supervisor then grows more and more angry with Mrs P's therapist and more and more inclined to intrude on the therapeutic work. In addition, the supervisee may sometimes talk about the therapist or the therapy. A supervisee may appropriately mention that it is difficult to work with a client who is afraid of cancer because he is going through his own fear of dying of cancer in his therapy. This point of contact is helpful, but there are other sorts of overlap that may cause much more conscious or unconscious difficulty. For example, Mrs P says, 'I decided to give the client a hug because that is what my therapist does'. Obviously this can be discussed in relation to the client and the kind of work being offered. It may also lead to judgement of the therapist by the supervisor. If the judgement is negative or dubious, it may lead to an unconscious condemnation of the supervisee: how can this person do good work if his therapy is dubious?

Therapy of the supervisee is also a fruitful ground for conflicts to arise for the supervisee between the values of the supervisor and the values of his or her therapist. Usually, one would hope that these values could be brought into the open and discussed. A supervisee may say, 'I did what my therapist would have done, but I know it's not what you would do'. I have to find out whether that is true first of all, and also decide how to deal with the possible conflict.

Often the conflict is over technique and yet fundamental values may reside in the choice of technique. Recently a therapist was expressing a conflict because her therapist is very open and willing to answer questions and make personal revelations. One way of working usually implies interpreting rather than answering or reacting immediately. With an area of technique such as the acceptability of touch, the difference will be obvious and may be able to be addressed. It does of course represent a difference of theory and inevitably, beneath that, a difference of values. Not touching could imply an overvaluing of the mind as opposed to the body. It could more constructively imply an orientation which stresses the development of the capacity for thought and reflection as opposed to gratification. In any case, a supervisee is likely to be greatly influenced by what he or she has grown used to in therapy. If the supervisor appears to disapprove of the therapist, that may cause damage just where the therapist is most in need of the possibility of useful work. Sometimes, however, the supervisee is ashamed of what his or her therapist does, wishes to treasure it in secret and will not expose it to the potential harsh judgement of the supervisor. This may or may not arise from a realistic assessment of what the supervisor actually thinks. Often these areas of conflict remain hidden unless a particularly difficult client brings them unavoidably to the surface. Secrets that are felt to be guilty may arise and lead to confused or ineffectual supervision.

The supervisor's relationship with the supervisor's consultant

The concept of supervising supervision is relatively new to psychotherapy although the British Association for Counselling requires it for the supervision of counsellors and most supervision trainings would also require it. It is discussed in Chapter 9 from a theoretical and technical point of view, but we would like to note here the way in which its increased relational complexity allows for greater resonance and complexity of values and ethical systems. At the most obvious level, the supervisor at the end of the chain has an ethical responsibility for what he or she knows is happening all the way down the line, but may have a primary duty to the immediate relationship with the supervisor presenting work. This is fine while all is going well, but may become difficult to manage when conflicts of values arise at any point in the complex structure.

The supervisor's relationship with society

The outside circle on the diagram is to represent the enclosing arms of the social and cultural context in which the supervision takes place. More specifically, supervision is often taking place within or on behalf of an agency or institution. Many supervisors are paid for or funded by the NHS, a GP practice or a training body. Some are working within the context of a private company or a voluntary body such as a charity. Each of these will set its own ethical standards, and conflicts will arise from the choices of priorities and duties that must be made.

The supervision may take place in the context of a private practice where there is no responsible body other than the therapist's and supervisor's training organisations and registering bodies. These gaze with a watchful parental eye, increasingly so as complaints and media interest in our shortcomings force themselves on our attention. Whatever the institutional context, we are all limited and shaped by social and political assumptions and norms. The supervisor works within a society that is undecided about the value of psychotherapy or counselling; that has no consensus about the importance of religion; that is still fighting over the meaning of political correctness and the damage done by language.

Samuels (1993) has developed our understanding of the psychotherapist's relationship to the political psyche of his clients, and of course the supervisor might well consider the effect of his or her own political convictions on the work. In addition, the political and social context determines such questions as who can be seen for psychotherapy (Clarkson, 1996). We will come back to the ethics of assessment later, but there is research which indicates the difficulty for ethnic minorities in reaching the therapy that might benefit them. We also know of the ethical problems involved in financial disenfranchisement of large numbers of people. Eurocentrism of both theory and technique is an issue which must be of concern to supervisors as well as to psychotherapists (Clarkson and Nippoda, 1997).

Conflicts in supervision

Having mapped out the territory in terms of depth and the overlapping circles of influence, we come now to look at some of the specific kinds of conflict that arise in supervision. The diagram in Figure 8.1 has one great advantage: it shows clear boundaries. These are of course metaphorical and illusional. In reality one of our areas of greatest difficulty, but also of the most potential for growth and development, is in drawing and shaping boundaries that are sufficiently firm to feel safe for the self, but sufficiently flexible to allow contact with another.

If we begin with the therapist/supervisor relationship itself, we can see that much has been written on the main aspects of the supervisory relationship and the dangers of over emphasising one role at the expense of others. The supervisor must not become the friend, the therapist or the teacher too much, not allowing any element of those roles to become dominant or the supervision itself will be contaminated. Each of these roles has its theoretical and technical problems, and each also has an ethical dimension. To take the possibility of friendship with a supervisee first, some regard supervision as a refreshing change from the clearer and more rigorous boundaries of therapy itself. With a supervisee one may ask ordinary social questions: 'How are you?' might be permissible, might be regarded as a necessary enquiry in order to assess how the work is likely to be done. This is a small example of the way in which the different tone of supervision may inhabit a grey area between therapy and something much closer to friendship, even when one is working with trainees. As the supervision proceeds along the spectrum to where one is working with colleagues who are themselves experienced therapists, the question of how much friendship is ethical becomes more and more difficult. Ethics cannot be divorced from a theoretical rationale, of course.

Ethical principles in the practice of psychotherapy are derived from various sources: the Judaeo-Christian tradition of ethical absolutes modified by utilitarian principles of the greatest good of the greatest number. These principles themselves have to be filtered through the understanding of the instinctual wishes and impulses that we have derived from psychoanalysis and analytical psychology. We would be unlikely to say that something is wrong from an ethical point of view if it was clearly for the good of the client and therapist and did not affect anyone else adversely. When it comes to friendship or social relationships between supervisor and therapist, we have on the one hand the imperative that says something like 'love ye one another'. On the other hand, we have to see transference and parallel process, and those may not show unless there is a fairly blank screen to reflect them. That is a theoretical reason to maintain a clear boundary. Other reasons deriving from ethical traditions would be similar to those governing other professions where it is not acceptable to provide professional services to friends or family. Judgement is clouded by emotional involvement and where unpleasant decisions must be made, a close emotional tie will make them more difficult if not impossible. It is difficult enough to disentangle the supervisor's countertransference response to the supervisee's from that to the client's material, without adding in the complications of a close or social relationship to the supervisee. Looking at the close links between theory and ethics, we inevitably see the difficulty of making any judgements about colleagues and friends supervising each other.

Many experienced therapists form pairs or small groups for supervision and work together for many years so that they know each other very well. Clearly this is a very different kind of supervision from supervising trainees. It would be foolish to say that it is unethical or unhelpful. On the other hand, it requires some discipline to make it bite. The group or the pair presumably need to ask each other from time to time whether they are sufficiently critical and perceptive of each other's weaknesses. Guggenbuhl-Craig (1971) comes to the conclusion that the only thing that will save us from identification with the archetype of the charlatan or the charismatic leader is the honest appraisal of friends.

Perhaps, therefore, there is room for friendship in supervision if it already exists and is used well. On the other hand, if it is introduced into a supervisory relationship to satisfy the therapist's erotic or narcissistic needs it is unethical and may well decrease the scope for useful parallel process or for necessary constructive criticism. Supervision often gives us trouble with our position in relation to the archetypes of the wise old man or woman, as well as the charlatan or leader. We all like to be admired, respected, as the experienced colleague or the teacher. Again, we would all agree that a supervisor may employ some teaching techniques and, particularly in training supervision, has some responsibility to pass on ideas, theoretical knowledge, reading and so on and to try to bring out the best from supervisees.

On the other hand, the supervisor needs to resist the temptation to enjoy the teaching function too much. The supervision can become a seminar in which there is a mutual enjoyment of intellectual discussion. Technically this would cease to be useful supervision because it would be unlikely to lead to helpful developments of the therapy for the client. Ethically it is problematic because the supervisor's task is to develop the therapist as a therapist in all respects. The supervisor may be modelling only one aspect of what a therapist needs to be and, undoubtedly, paral-

lel process working backwards may lead to a restricted functioning in
the therapy. Since all supervisors must presumably themselves be therapists, there is always a pull towards becoming the therapist of the supervisee. The boundary between the two is often difficult to see and to
maintain but it needs constant vigilance. We have come across fairly
dramatic crossings of this boundary.

Recently a supervisee came saying that she needed supervision
because her previous supervisor had been so interested in her and so
uninterested in her clients that they had both decided that she had
better go to him for therapy and find another supervisor. This requires
suspended judgement. What is coming across is a blurred boundary and
a failure of the supervisory responsibility. This has to be held in suspen-
sion because it is only a second-hand account, as always. At least the
nature of the relationship was understood and the important thing is
always to make it conscious and clear to both parties.

The opposite tendency is revealed by a different example. A trainee
had need of extra supervision and reported that his therapist had
offered to supervise some client work. This also would have been separate from the therapy time and would have been presumably clearly
distinct to both people, but the ethical question remains: is it possible
to be, in this literal way, both therapist and supervisor? The answer
seems to be that if the work is psychodynamic at all, and transference
and countertransference are used, two relationships at once would be
confusing to say the least. It is also important to note that to conduct a
therapy relationship and a supervisory relationship at the same time
with the same person contravenes the BAC Code of Ethics for supervisors (B 1.6). Boundaries are important in individual relationships; they
are, if anything, even more contentious within organisations or institutions carrying out counselling or psychotherapy.

Conflicts over boundaries are bound to arise if there is any overlapping
of supervision and line management. A line manager is unlikely to be able
to maintain the boundary between the needs of the organisation and the
needs of the client. Confidentiality is also likely to be difficult to maintain.
Managers need to manage waiting lists and throughput and will want to
know the reasons why certain clients need more time. A supervisor is often
the person who has to hold the difficult interface between the pressures of
time and money on the one hand and an assessment of the benefit that
may be possible on the other. This is an unenviable place to be.
Psychiatrists are often unwilling to leave therapists and supervisors to go at
their own pace and may, because of the pressures that they themselves are
under, seek to know more of the detail of the therapy than is appropriate.

Training organisations provide some of the most difficult boundary
problems in that they demand assessment of trainees. The supervisor's
assessment is often the most important element in a training and carries
the most weight. Assessing trainees is a skilled and demanding job but

is something that most supervisors have to pick up either from their own internalised experience or from other experience such as teaching. There are profound ethical questions involved.

A frequent conflict is between the need or wish to give the dubious trainee time to develop and the question of whether he or she is actually depriving clients of a better experience with another therapist. This is inevitably a difficult question to answer as it brings us up against the inevitable lack of direct knowledge of the client. Nevertheless, a trainee may show the same difficulties with a number of clients, as long as the training requires that a number of clients must be seen. If the lack of progress and helpfulness shows itself in several cases, the supervisor may well have grounds to draw the boundary and say that this person is not good enough at the work to continue.

Useful questions that tend to bring out the essentials are:
- Is the trainee able to give this client the opportunity to develop further?
and when it is a question of qualification:
- would you refer patients to this person?

The issues raised by assessment are of course numerous. Much of the responsibility will be held by the training organisation concerned, but supervisors will still have their own consciences and their own professional responsibility.

The supervisor's responsibility

One of the major ethical problems for supervisors is to determine the extent and the limits of the supervisor's responsibility.

We envisage the responsibility of the supervisor to lie in four main areas:

- for assessment and management of the client
- for competence and ethical/professional behaviour of the psychotherapist
- to the organisation that employs or sponsors the therapy, society at large
- to the profession as a whole.

Within these four main spheres, there is a great deal of room for debate about how far the supervisor can and should be responsible. There is of course a difference between the supervisor of a trainee or of an employee within an organisation where there is a clear contractual responsibility, and the supervisor of a qualified and experienced therapist. We could simply say that the contract between supervisor and therapist must make clear the extent and limits of responsibility. This is important and there should be some sort of contract and understanding, but whenever a difficulty arises, there is likely to be a problem in interpreting the contract and deciding just what the supervisor will do and say. In the first areas, for example, the supervisor will presumably hear about the assessment of clients.

Trainees may not have freedom of choice about whom they see and may not be doing the actual assessments. More experienced therapists, on the other hand, are probably assessing their own clients and deciding whether or not to see a difficult client. This is precisely the sort of case that is most likely to be brought to the supervisor.

The following is an example of the kind of case where the supervisor may feel responsible for what happens and will have to decide whether in fact he or she does has any responsibility beyond facilitating the supervisee.

A fairly experienced, qualified therapist brought an assessment to discuss. The client was a man of 43, subject to fits of rage at work and at home. He said that he wants to be a better husband and father. He had been to Relate for a few sessions and said that he found it quite helpful because 'it got my wife off my back for a while'. Recently he had begun to hit his wife again.

The history was problematic. He had very little memory of it but had been told by his brother that he was neglected by his mother who preferred the older daughter and found boys a problem. The father had left home when the client was 2 or 3. He remembered best the years from 16 to 20 when he went round with a football gang. He had been convicted of four offences involving violence but none so serious that he was given a custodial sentence. He was fined and cautioned.

He settled down after he got married to a strong woman, but he says that he finds it difficult to be what she wants him to be and particularly to talk to her. She has urged him to come for therapy. The therapist is deeply ambivalent. She is a woman of about 55 and not easily frightened. She says that she was struck by this patient's red hair and the fact that he never made eye contact. She says 'I can't make out whether he is just not used to being open, or whether there is really something for me to be frightened about'. There are indications that he is motivated to work but also questions about what kind of transference might be created with an older woman. In a bright and somewhat dismissive way, the therapist brushes the problems to one side and says 'Well, I'll take him on. I think it'll be all right and I think he has potential to use this kind of work'.

The supervisor may see it as his or her job simply to support the therapist or perhaps to go more deeply into the ambivalence. How far does the responsibility, both for the client and the therapist, go? If the supervisor's countertransference experience of the client is negative and disturbing, would it be right to refuse to ask the therapist not to take the client or even to refuse to supervise him? What if the supervisor is very doubtful that a particular client can make use of psychoanalytic work at all?

In this case, the therapist confessed to having omitted to make any sort of trial interpretation or to have forgotten the outcome of whatever was said. Not only does assessment raise questions about the responsibility of the supervisor, there are many ongoing matters of management and technique that we all face frequently. Clients who are suicidal, potentially psychotic, severely regressed or physically ill all raise difficult questions and can put enormous strain on the supervisor's trust of the therapist. The temptation may well be to take too much responsibility and tell the therapist what to do. This may be the safest policy, but is it supervision?

On the other hand, there is an unresolved question about the supervisor's legal responsibility. As far as the law is concerned in the UK at the moment, there is no definitive answer as supervisor involvement in, for example, a tort of negligence or a criminal offence has not been tested. Legal opinion, however, is that a supervisor could be an accessory. It therefore behoves us to take reasonable care for the well-being, not only of the client but of others who may potentially be harmed.

Supervisors, like other citizens, may well find themselves with knowledge that is difficult or dangerous either to use or to suppress. Clearly, a satisfactory supervisory relationship will allow these sorts of questions to be worked through so that the resulting practice will be the consensus of both supervisor and therapist. As long as this is the case, ethical codes and codes of practice will simply be part of the background and will inform but not need to dominate practice. Under the pressure of a stressful or difficult problem, however, the consensus may break down. The therapist may do or fail to do what the supervisor thinks is essential. What does the supervisor do if the therapist fails, for example, to get the client to speak to the GP or to deal satisfactorily with possible child abuse? As in the therapeutic relationship, the first priority is to have the client or therapist to deal with the problem him or herself, but if that does not or cannot happen, then the supervisor may have to take responsibility and require certain action.

Organisational contexts

Taking responsibility may be helped if the work is being done within an organisation. A supervisor may then be able to discuss the difficulty with a legitimate source of authority such as the head of a clinic or service and two people may then share the decision that needs to be made. On the other hand, organisations may require that supervisors take responsibility for such matters as reducing waiting lists, limiting the amount of time that any given client may have in therapy.

Overt or covert racism and prejudice may influence the availability and quality of client care and supervision. Working with supervisees and clients from a different ethnic or cultural background raises questions of awareness, personal values and discriminatory practice for the supervisor (BAC, 1995: B 1.9). Such differences may range from gender to sexual practices to class. Arguments can be heard that mixed race supervisory relationships are inadvisable on the grounds that there is always a cultural power imbalance, or on the theoretical issue that psychoanalytic theory is inherently Eurocentric. Whatever the supervisor's views, he or she may need to be aware of the range of opinions and the need for addressing issues of difference very seriously (López, 1997).

The financial difficulties of the organisation will also impact on supervision, either indirectly through client input or directly in, for example, limiting the amount of supervision available so that too many clients must be covered in too little time. Where supervision is in any way affected by managerial issues such as training opportunities, promotion, resource allocation, status or any other such factor of threat or reward, quality client supervision may become impossibly compromised in terms of authenticity, honesty and risk.

Organisational support may make some supervisory decisions easier or at least inevitable, but the supervisor will still be left with some of the most difficult problems. When a therapist is ill, or becomes incompetent, in some cases only a supervisor may know of practice that is unsafe or inadequate. On the other hand, when therapists are incompetent they are likely to avoid supervisors altogether, or hide the nature of the work that is being done.

Professional responsibility

One of the most difficult areas for many supervisors is to insist on detailed accounts of work with clients so that there is some chance of judging what the practice is like. Even if you are fairly sure that you are hearing the detail of what is going on, there is no easy way of judging where work that you do not like or do not approve of has become so bad as to be incompetent or unethical. A supervisor may have to judge whether it is better to continue supervising someone in the hope of improving the practice or whether he or she can no longer be associated with the work that is being done. If that point is reached, the supervisor may have to report the therapist to a professional body, and that is one of the most difficult things for anyone to do.

Under the heading of responsibility to colleagues and profession, supervisors must obviously consider whether a therapist's practice is likely to bring the profession into disrepute. Is it fair to land supervisors with this kind of guardianship role? Many of us have non-judgemental tendencies and have chosen this profession out of a desire to be neither a powerful participant nor totally a bystander (Clarkson, 1996). Often we find it contrary to both inclination and training to take responsibility for another. We still have to ask ourselves whether we can take on the role of supervisor if we are not prepared to take some responsibility. An example of this sort of difficulty has come to our notice. A therapist has been hospitalised for mental illness but has recovered sufficiently to be discharged. The therapist wishes to see his clients as soon as possible. The supervisor is the only person who is in a position to say whether or not the therapist is fit to practise. A more common experience is bereavement, where the therapist is obviously not functioning as well as usual; but where exactly do we draw the line and say that he or she must not work, especially as in many cases work is providing a form of therapy for the therapist?

Most supervisors will, sooner or later, come across a problem with a supervisee which is not solved within the normal supervisory process. The avenues of discussion have been tried and suggested improvements or changes have been ignored. What happens then? According to recent research (Clarkson and Lindsay, 1997; Lindsay and Clarkson, 1997) the second ranking source of dilemmas for UKCP psychotherapists was colleagues' conduct. This indicates that supervisors are likely to come across conduct in supervisees which they cannot condone. The codes would require that the supervisor either makes a complaint against the therapist to the relevant professional body or at least transfers him or her to another supervisor. This does not often happen in practice. We could all see reasons for this. Supervisees are a part of a practice and there are economic and conservative motives to keep the same person and hope that there will be some improvement.

Rationalising may also go on along the lines that the person needs time to improve, or is perhaps not quite as much at fault as may have appeared. Fundamentally, we are reluctant to invoke a disciplinary procedure or make any sort of complaint against a colleague. A supervisor understands only too well that a complaint would have to be well substantiated and the process would be time consuming and disturbing. We can certainly hope that the occasions on which there would be any question of such action would be rare, but perhaps supervisors need to be willing to accept that they do have a responsibility to the profession when they cannot find any way of amending a psychotherapist's work.

References

BAC (1995) *Code of Ethics for Supervisors*. Rugby: British Association for Counselling.

Clarkson, P. (1996) *The Bystander (An End to Innocence in Human Relationships?)* London: Whurr.

Clarkson, P. (1997) Supervision in counselling, psychotherapy and health: An intervention priority sequencing model, *European Journal for Counselling, Psychotherapy and Health*, 1(1).

Clarkson, P. and Lindsay, G. (1997) Ethical dilemmas of UKCP psychotherapists – comparisons of results from similar APA and BPS studies, *The Psycotherapist* (accepted for publication).

Clarkson, P. and Murdin, L. (1996) When rules are not enough: the letter and spirit of the law. *Counselling* 7(1): 31–35.

Clarkson, P. and Nippoda, Y. (1997) Cross-cultural Issues in Counselling Psychology Practice: A qualitative study of one multicultural training organisation, in P. Clarkson (ed.) *Counselling Psychology: Integrating Theory, Research and Supervised Practice*, London: Routledge. pp 95–118.

Guggenbuhl-Craig, A. (1971) *Power in the Helping Professions*. Dallas, TX: Spring Publications.

Lindsay, G. and Clarkson, P. (1997) Ethical dilemmas of psychotherapists, submitted for publication in *The Psycotherapist*.

López, S.R. (1997) Cultural Competence in Psychotherapy: A Guide for Clinicians and their Supervisors, in Watkins, C.E. Jr. (ed.) *Handbook of Psychotherapy Supervision*, New York: Wiley.

Samuels, A. (1993) *The Political Psyche*. London: Routledge.

Chapter 9
An intervention priority sequencing model for supervision

PETRŪSKA CLARKSON

Reviewing the vast literature on the practice and learning of supervision (e.g. Watkins, 1997) one is impressed by the enormous volume of opinions, models, research studies, and studies of research studies on the one hand and the comparatively sparse fruits from this decades-long endeavour for the participant, practitioner or teacher of supervision.

Ellis and Ladany (1997) typically write:

> Conceivably, the most telling implication of this review [of research findings] is for practitioners to be extremely cautious and skeptical of the empirical literature we have reviewed. There are few practical implications of the research reviewed here. The research suggests that the quality of the supervisory relationship is paramount to successful supervision. (p. 495)

For reviewing the values and vectors of the supervisory relationship over a period of time, the Supervision Relationship Model might be the most suitable model drawn from my work. This is based on extensive qualitative research (Clarkson, 1990, 1995) which has resulted in the identification and utilisation of five kinds of therapeutic relationship common across all the major approaches to psychotherapy. These are:

- the **working alliance**
- the **transference/countertransference** relationship
- the **reparative** or **developmentally needed** relationship
- the **person-to-person** relationship
- the **transpersonal** relationship.

To become skilful in using (and, what is more, teaching or supervising) any of these or other models of supervision demands in-depth study and extensive supervised practice and supervision of supervision. The preliminary point here is to validate using a variety of tools and models available to supervisors to create a professional world rich in variety, creativity and flexibility (Clarkson, 1995).

Furthermore, we should endeavour to match the model to the purpose. For example, my Bands of Supervision Model (Clarkson, 1992) is best suited for teaching supervision while my Supervision Assessment Model (Clarkson, 1992) is more useful for the assessment of supervision and learning how to assess one's own and others' supervision in a short space of time according to quite definite criteria.

Developing range and flexibility in using different models for different people at different times is perhaps a more inspiring objective than adapting to the demands of one 'right' model. Whether or not the 'supervisory philosophy and structure' was appropriate can be judged by the demands of the situation, rather than the precision of replicating one single 'right' model – whatever we may conceive that to be (Doherty, 1991). The most important quality in a trainer or a supervisor is probably the desire to continue learning rather than the achievement of 'being right' defined by only some external criteria. The findings of my research with Aviram (Clarkson and Aviram, 1997) provide another empirically based conceptual model for comparison or integration.

The purpose of this chapter is unashamedly utilitarian and practical. The Priority Sequencing Model presented here has developed from some 25 years' experience as a consultant supervisor and teacher of counselling, psychology and psychotherapy in multiple approaches and settings. The justification for presenting it rests solely on the numerous novice and experienced practitioners and supervisors who have found it extremely helpful in their everyday practice where the pressures of finding one's way through the multifaceted complexities of the therapeutic relationship hone effectiveness in a very direct manner.

Prioritising interventions in the supervisory field

The intervention-prioritising framework discussed here was specifically developed as a conceptual map to help supervisees and supervisors in an immediate way. It is of particular value in locating *where* a problem is likely to be focused and *how* to direct the supervisory effort more effectively within the usually limited periods of time devoted to professional development, maintenance or support.

There is so much to comprehend – the conscious relationship between (at least) three pairs of people (patient/analyst, analyst/supervisor, supervisor/patient), the unconscious relationship between each of them, the diagonal relationships between them in terms of mutual awareness (or not) of each other's unconscious material and motivations, the relationship of each one between the conscious and unconscious dimensions of their own contribution to the interaction. Of course, there is also the interplay of all of these with the specific professional or training organisation or institution on the one hand (Carr, 1995) and the larger forces of life and collective evolution on the other.

Counselling and psychotherapy supervision are such complex fields that the more one learns, the more options for action open up. Contemporary economic and professional conditions often demand that we all need to produce more in less time. One of the greatest challenges for supervisors is to quickly, efficiently, appropriately and helpfully prioritise for attention or action the material brought to the supervisory relationship.

Taking the next decision (of responding or not responding, questioning, supporting, challenging, clarifying, reflecting, facilitating, catalysing, modelling, structuring or interpreting) can get increasingly difficult for any supervisor. Often, the greater one's understanding of the complexity of the situations and – sometimes – of the life-and-death issues which are the daily bread of people in this profession, the greater the range of choices, decisions and understandings which inform the supervisory process. It used to be the case that supervision was considered a natural result of experience as an analyst, but recent developments have shown an increasing recognition of the role and value of training and supervision for supervisors.

As the field of supervision grows and develops it also becomes clear that there is only so much to which one can pay attention in any given period of time. Of all the many choices facing supervisors, one of the most strategically important is probably *how to prioritise* – what is most important in a specific situation, how to select what to do next, to which factors to give most urgent attention. In a way, the operational imperative is which figure to select for attention from the dynamically fluctuating background of often competing and frequently conflicting possibilities.

The Intervention Priority Sequencing Model

To make the choices of where to focus most economically and efficiently for supervision, and deciding priorities for supervisory attention, the Danger, Confusion, Conflict, Deficit and Development Model may be suitable and beneficial. It is also extremely effective for decision-making hierarchies in crisis intervention situations, whether these be natural disasters or psychiatric emergencies occurring in the context of conferences.

In particular it is efficient and useful because its use can often prevent or reduce wastage of time and effort, thus increasing efficiency and effectiveness. Many counsellors and psychotherapists of course also use it for therapy planning and anticipating twists and turnings along the therapeutic journey. It has also proved valuable for the training and supervision of supervisors, trainers and consultants. (See also Clarkson, 1992; Clarkson and Kellner, 1995, regarding applications.)

At any given moment the supervisory focus may involve any part of the supervisory system ranging from the inner world of the client to current events affecting the cultural assumptions of an organisation. Although detailed consideration of how any part of the supervisory system can be chosen to be the focus for an intervention is precluded here for reasons of space, it is possible to show some examples from a variety of situations for explanatory purposes. Specific applications are left to the individual reader and future publications.

Figure 9.1. Overlapping supervisory systems (this is a version of a diagram first published in Clarkson, 1997c)

Of course any diagrammatic representation of systems or subsystems involved in the supervisory field, such as Figure 9.1, is never truly independent. Each can represent the whole at certain epistemological, metaphysical or narrative levels. The notions of supervisory fractals (Clarkson, 1993) or parallel process (Searles, 1955; Clarkson, 1997b) both indicate ways in which whatever part is detailed for attention or intervention, the effects will be system-wide. However, in this instance the signals are sorted into five categories primarily concerned with:

- **danger** (some threat in the system)
- **confusion** (some loss of focus in the system)
- **conflict** (some split, polarisation or conflict in the system)
- **deficit** (some experience of need or deprivation or for reparation)
- **development** (some requirement to increase depth, breadth or complexity).

When we think about supervision as a system, this framework suggests that any disturbance can be classified in at least these five major ways. This framework provides a way of thinking about the supervisory system which enables the psychotherapist and the supervisor jointly to explore, contract and evaluate interventions. The categories represent a sequence which can maximise effectiveness in making supervisory interventions.

The Priority Sequencing Model has an underlying and invariable order if it is to be used successfully. Work needs to be done usually *in this order of clearance* if it is to be effective. Perhaps most of the impasses in therapy, consultancy and supervision can be traced to having skipped one or more of these sequential steps.

Danger

Where any part of the client/therapist system is in perceived danger, the conscious or unconscious preoccupation of the system is with *survival issues*. These will tend to bind or cathect the libidinal energy so as to make work with other themes ineffective. Therapeutic or supervisory issues concerning homicide, suicide, psychosis, risk to others and ethical concerns almost always need to be dealt with first. Since the Tarasoff case (see Thompson, 1990), psychotherapeutically involved professionals are even more aware of their duties to third parties and the other dangers constituted by our professions.

People cannot engage in learning, developing or healing effectively if they feel endangered at any level – and this includes moral endangerment, as in collusion with crime, deceit or abuse. When the supervision is used for any other reason than to deal with this perceived danger or to develop plans, strategies and resources to cope with it, avoid it or transform it, the effort will probably be wasted, since the key issue for focal concern will have been missed. One can be working with a supervisee for quite a long while, getting nowhere, before it emerges, for example, that she is physically so afraid of a homicidal client that she could not think at all.

If safety is endangered (consciously or unconsciously) there is little energy left for anything but defensive behaviour to avoid collapse or flight. Even in supervision, human biological needs usually take priority. To the extent that these needs are denied or avoided, no significant other work can be accomplished in the therapy or the supervision. Sometimes danger can be overestimated, as in the example of the group psychotherapist who (as it transpired, falsely) felt that a group member was a spy for the totalitarian government and potentially endangering not only the work of the group but also the survival of that organisation in that particular country. The fact is that until such danger issues are attended to, the work of the group cannot truly progress.

Whether supervisory issues are presented as confusion ('help me sort this out'), conflict ('help me resolve this conflict') or deficit ('give me x, y or z which I need') it is vital to separate out relevant danger issues and deal with them first. When there is the presence or potential for danger it is important to listen, to acknowledge the feelings, to explore the sources of the danger, assess their reality and deal with the nature of the danger as well as the potential for retrieving or developing resources to deal with it. These may in fact involve management issues such as admission to hospital, referral to another practitioner, or calling the police.

There may sometimes be a temptation for the supervisor to teach when the people are not ready to learn, or to reassure when such reassurance would be false. A therapist may also attempt to draw the supervisor into 'rescuing' them – taking their responsibility away from them rather than enabling them to deal with the threats to their clinical, professional or organisational survival in a realistic way.

The survival issue may not always be as the therapist or supervisor perceives it. In counselling and therapy it is essential to question all our assumptions as culturally biased. For example, for many women from certain African cultures the fear of being rejected by marriageable men outweighs the dangers of contracting AIDS. Airhihenbuwa *et al.* (1992) show that, for the women, to be rejected as a result of their insisting on condom use is a more immediate and palpable danger than potential death from the disease.

To the inexperienced and economically dependent counsellor, financial danger regarding the mortgage and children's education may result in an ill-considered rejection of brief therapies, a refusal to confront ethical and professional misconduct in professionals making referrals to them and also in keeping on clients who need far more experienced or specialised care than they can actually provide.

Confusion

Issues to do with confusion and contamination need to be dealt with next. Unconscious transference, countertransference and projective identification phenomena can become pervasive and crippling. *Learning and healing requires confusion to be dispersed.* Deconfusing the issues precedes work with conflict. The value of and means for separating out different universes of discourse has been discussed by authors such as Gilbert Ryle (1966) and also in my epistemological seven-level model (Clarkson, 1975).

Cultural assumptions can increase confusion and misdiagnosis. A black man was diagnosed as schizophrenic in a South African hospital on the basis of his 'hearing voices'. It was only when a young psychiatric registrar asked him what the voices were saying, that it became clear that 'the voices' were the intercom calls for doctors and nurses to different wards: 'Calling Dr Smith, will Dr Smith please come to ward 6'!

A supervisory system suffering from confusion has difficulty identifying priorities or achieving high focus. High focus is classically associated with higher likelihood of effectiveness of outcome. Where confusion reigns, it may even be difficult to identify the problem. The supervisory system does not know what information is relevant. Prejudices about childhood history or theory are not examined or tested (McNamee and Gergen, 1992). In the confused supervisory system, feelings are often presented as facts. For example, a therapist may be convinced that because 'this person is a borderline' certain procedures will not be effective. The supervisor will notice these and many other signs of confusion.

When a supervisor is unclear about what the task is, or when the therapist is confused about client goals, there is a general sense of disorientation and lack of direction. This is obviously not a good time to deal with conflict or to provide input or teaching. Often the supervisor may feel that the therapist wants or needs this. The supervisor's task is to restrain premature action, and to help to clarify the issues, roles and relationships, including authority and expertise issues. It is also important to provide interpretation, analysis, models and maps to facilitate the exploration of options and choices, and consequent assessment of the impact of possible alternative interventions.

Engaging in conflict resolution when the supervisor/therapist system is unclear about the nature, consequences and significance of conflict is also a waste of time and effort. It is vital that the supervisor finds some way of dealing with any danger experienced by the system first. They may then engage with clarifying confusion – without getting drawn into premature attempts to resolve conflict (this is bound to fail), or premature attempts to provide replenishing or corrective experiences (except those that help people clarify confusion). These are likely to be wasteful and not as effective as if the system had been adequately prepared to receive and use the resources which are provided.

When a supervisory system is in a confused state it is most important not to get sucked into that confusion. Most supervisors have experienced the rapidity and persuasiveness with which they can be drawn into sharing the feeling of confusion and an atmosphere of inability to sort it out which is characteristic of some therapist/client systems. At the same time there may be a temptation to oversimplify and reduce the confusion artificially by accepting only one frame of reference, or getting into an argument about the best way forward – thereby creating more conflict before the system is ready to deal with it.

What may appear as accidental insulin mismanagement, for example, may in fact be masking a deep-seated suicidal intention – work devoted to confusion in the supervisory system may entirely miss the danger.

Indeed, it could as effectively preclude appropriate intervention. A counsellor who either through ignorance of the symptoms or nervousness about consulting the 'establishment doctors' about counselling patients may not notice severe and increasing signs indicating a neurological investigation – thus continuing in counselling while a massive brain tumour is wreaking irredeemable damage. Working with empathy, interpretation or dialogue on repetitive headaches, unusual visual disturbances and increasing loss of balance are examples of working with deficit, confusion or conflict as foci, and missing the danger.

Sometimes working with confusion alone can be sufficient to resolve a problem quickly and easily, e.g. resolving a misunderstanding of instructions about birth control, understanding and using a hospital's patient charter, or the difference between psychiatrists and psychotherapists, or forming an interpretation which allows a lesbian woman to withdraw a projection on to her doctor of her authoritative father and question his misdiagnosis of her premenstrual tension as sexual frustration.

Conflict

Once clarification has been achieved, it is more probable that conflict resolution, mediation, integration or mutual respect for difference can be accomplished. Attempts to work with conflict before the previous stages have been done often fail. We need to be clear about the protagonists in a conflict and about what issues the conflict is actually being conducted. Much unnecessary blood has been spilled and lives ruined because of people or countries engaging in conflict or wars before clarifying what was at stake.

It is not too difficult to diagnose when the therapist/client system is in conflict. It is more difficult to ensure that such conflicts are clearly understood by all involved. Conflict issues tend to be characterised by splits, a great amount of energetic activity, categorically different positions, failure of all reasonable attempts to negotiate, an unwillingness to compromise, and some combination of active acting out or passive aggressive behaviour by any or all of the parties.

If the supervisor has satisfied themself and, importantly, also the participants that there is no real danger in exploring, clarifying or engaging with the conflict, it is possible to begin to use it. The conflict can then become a source of enhanced creativity; anger, aggression and difference can enable everybody affected by the system more effectively and creatively.

There is often a myth that therapist/client systems are more successful when there is no conflict or even implicit disagreement. In fact, the existence – even the celebration – of conflict can be a profound spur to creativity, innovation and resilience. In therapy 'empathic failures' (Kohut, 1977) or 'therapeutic errors' can provide the points of breakthrough as much as breakdown (Safran, 1993). However, the genuine fruitful engagement with conflict can only happen if

- there is no experience of danger; for example, if there are no damaging consequences of expressing and standing up for different views
- the system is not experiencing confusion; for example, if there is not widespread vagueness or incapacitating bewilderment about exactly what the issues or the subsystems involved are.

It may be important for the supervisor to learn the history of the conflict in order to discover, for example, whether it is primarily a personality type clash (e.g. an extrovert therapist imposing their notions of mental health on an introverted intuitive) or whether the protagonists are interested in common values and the productive outcome to the benefit of all. To gain from the benefits of conflict, it is important that the supervisor models effective conflict handling – welcomes it, tries to understand it, and works towards resolution. The most important task is to show how it can be productively used.

The supervisor can become a model and help the therapist/client system to understand conflict and transform it into effective and creative problem-solving. Therapist/client systems are often in need of learning or improving their abilities to manage conflict. Providing an arena for the conflict to be surfaced, examined or rehearsed is most valuable. Then the space, the time and the safety in which to pursue difference can lead towards integrating or coexistence – or a celebration of diversity and variety.

It is a common supervisor error to pathologise conflict – the therapist who is in conflict or conflictful may already feel sick or wrong. This often arises from the supervisor's own fear or denial of his or her own aggression or past trauma. Ignoring or minimising it reduces the possibility for learning from it and benefiting from the potential for enhanced creativity and better understanding which conflict brings in its way.

Neutrality is usually a good starting position as long as there is no danger of abuse by holding such neutrality. There are many situations where neutrality is in fact ill-disguised support for the aggressor – and the so-called helping professions are by no means exempt (Clarkson, 1995).

Common intrapsychic conflicts are the stuff of everyday life – and 'the psychopathology of everyday life' (Freud, 1960):
- wanting to give up smoking, but afraid that creativity will die in the process
- working too hard with high blood pressure, but reluctant to sacrifice what is felt as the life-enhancing adrenaline rushes of risky futures ventures
- knowing that exercise will help depression, yet feeling too down to move away from the TV.

Then there are conflicts at work, in the family, between friends and (of course) disagreements about implicit or explicit values as these affect counselling and psychotherapy every minute of the fifty-minute hour, the four-session managed care or the five-minute home visit.

Conflicts can be over-diagnosed, tackled prematurely (before the previous stages), displaced, or appear within the WOT (way of talking – Farrell, 1979) of the therapy as 'resistance' whereas sometimes violations are taking place, the dangers of which are irretrievable dangers to identity, integrity, community. These are too often overlooked, particularly when working with anyone who is not western European, educated and middle-class.

> Whatever their ideology, the majority of 'talk therapists' will see their individual clients as the main 'problem' . . . patients may have to *learn* this world view gradually acquiring with each session a further understanding of the concepts, symbols and vocabulary that comprise it. This can be seen as a form of 'acculturation' whereby they acquire a new mythic world couched, for example, in terms of the Freudian, Jungian, Kleinian or Laingian models. This mythic world, shared eventually by patient and therapist, is often inaccessible to the patient's family or community, who in any case are excluded from the consultation. (Helman, 1994: 280)

Deficit

Issues to do with replenishment of lacks, reparenting, knowledge or skill deficits, etc. are most likely to be effective if the previous stages have been cleared. In the last instance the therapist/client system can primarily be characterised as needing something – being in 'deficit'. If it is information about a specific approach which is needed, the provision of such a system will tend to be satisfying, satisfactory and comparatively easily accomplished. *Training or educational input which is provided to the therapist when the deficit is appropriately and accurately identified results in appropriate change in the client/therapist system.*

However, if helpful hints or useful strategies are brought in to give the therapist/client system something while that system is still experiencing conflict, confusion or a sense of danger, it is more than likely that the anticipated outcome will not materialise and unpleasant disillusionment and cynical responses are to be expected.

On one occasion a request for teaching on developmental theory (apparently meeting a need) coincided with a sudden reduction in the therapist's income. In this context, the request may have been coming from a position of confusion, or it may have been an attempt to deal with conflict about whether patients should be discouraged from terminating. It is likely that the therapist was experiencing danger, possibly in value conflict, and confused about their own future. Without taking these issues into account in contracting and designing this work, the supervision would not have been effective.

Strategic priorities when meeting a deficit are first to establish what people already have as resources, skills, training, and options before providing anything. It is also necessary to find out what worked before and, most importantly, to identify what went wrong before. This is to ensure that the supervisor is not working fruitlessly within one of the three previous areas of danger, confusion or conflict.

When one is as certain as possible that there is actually a deficit need, it becomes reasonably simple to follow the classic instructions to start from where the supervisor/client system is, establish their needs and wants, and provide and review their use of relevant input. It may be for the client to take the medication as prescribed or for the trainee to keep adequate records, or for the supervisor to display better empathic attunement.

A common mistake within this focus is to assume that there is a solution which can be provided by teaching. All the time-honoured admonishments against giving advice or information to clients or supervisees are grounded in the frequent and sometimes disastrous errors when deficit-filling interventions are delivered without having a sound enough working alliance and within a distorted and unresolved transference or countertransference reaction: 'I was assertive like you taught us, but when I hit the waiter over the head, they put me in prison', or 'I did what you told me and the client had a terrible relapse'.

Sometimes the deficit-focused intervention may result in a beneficial change, but not the desired improvement, because the intervention did not address the problems as experienced by the supervisees. Another common mistake is to 'do it' for the therapist/client system rather than enabling supervisees to find, use or discover their own resources.

However, on the other hand to deprive clients or supervisees from information, guidance or advice when it is clear that they need it and likely that they will be able to use it well if carefully delivered, can be simply an unethical prolonging of ignorance and distress (Boadella, 1988). A married man needed only one session to relieve him of the incapacitating guilt he felt for masturbating, by providing him with the statistical information available on how normal and ordinary it is for many married men to do this – even happily married men. For a supervisee worried about whether the client complaining of persecution was psychotically paranoid, a call to the GP and the local race relations office was all that was needed to confirm that there was vicious harassment on the client's housing estate.

Development

This supervisory focus concerns issues to do with *increasing complexity, effectiveness, capacity and an increase in range and flexibility of understandings, sensibilities and behavioural repertoire*. It is not meant to only refer to step-by-step hierarchical developmental models since these are often culture bound, but may include those alongside more cyclic models of professional enhancement (Clarkson, 1994) or the sudden and apparently unpredictable shifts which characterise post-mortem conceptualisations of evolutionary or quantum changes in complex systems. It is moving the mutual universes of discourse from simplex to complex to multiplex (Stewart, 1996).

Reviews of the research concerning supervisee development have, in any case, found such to be 'simplistic . . . not acceptably tested, and no tentative inferences from the data to the model seem justifiable given the inadequate rigor of the studies' (Ellis and Ladany, 1997, p. 483).

In terms of supervision, the notion of development is here, for example, referring to the learning edge or developmental stretch for the therapist/supervisor system – those issues which are not nurtured through avoidance (such as cultural implications, for example) or which are avoided because of ignorance or feeling overwhelmed and helpless (due to overpowering organisational forcefield influences) or even the blunting that comes from over-use and desensitisation.

An example of the latter is the phase of 'unconscious incompetence' which Robinson (1974) showed follows after the achievement of 'conscious competence'. This last sequel of achieved competency can, however, be transformed if the supervisor or supervisor's consultant repeatedly involves him/herself in a cycle of continuing education, questioning and research – even of the very assumptions on which they had based their practice and their teaching in the first place.

There is of course always the potential for development, but only rarely would it take priority over the previous foci in terms of importance or urgency – particularly as far as client need must take primacy. This is necessary and sometimes regrettable because these developmental edges may be the very sources of nourishment and creativity which keep a professional in these disciplines alive, questioning and vibrant. It is perhaps associated to the leisure in supervision which can be a prerequisite for creative growth, analogous to that for artistic development in a society.

When supervision is normally a rushed business, an attempt to cover too many patients in too little time, or to meet endless external 'requirements' rather than to burgeon as a professional in tune with the tides of a life in these disciplines, these aspects are pushed out and ignored at risk of the very joy, curiosity and creativity which often brought people to this work in the first place. Of course clients must come first. However, the care and nurture of the professional, whether novice or veteran, should accompany this priority if the supervisory system is not to become an empty hypocrisy.

When the supervisory system is in need of development (or when it is in need of the space or time to generate such development) the focus needs to be on learning what is generalisable to other situations, other clients, other supervisees. It may mean creating the space for new needs to emerge (Skevington, MacArthur and Somerset, 1997). It concerns metaphorically developing an aspirational arrow that is never satisfied with being good enough, but is always striving around questions such as 'What if this didn't work?' 'How would I know that something completely new for me might not be better?' 'What is the effect of this on the whole of society?' (Clarkson, 1996) or even 'How can I bring beauty, poetry, soul into this work ?' (Clarkson, 1997a).

Application

Using this framework for the subjective, feeling reality of the client/therapist system results in three sets of foci for supervisors:

- accurately diagnosing the supervisee's need as presented within the relevant subsystem
- understanding that the presenting problem may be only an acceptable way of requesting help on a different underlying issue of which the therapist may or may not be aware
- choosing an appropriate intervention or intervention strategy aligned to the focused psychological reality of the supervisor/therapist/client situation.

Accurate diagnosis relies on sensitive and accurate perception of relationships within the therapist/client system. This develops as the supervisor responds to the needs he or she perceives in the client, or experiences the therapist as having – this provides an initial diagnosis.

As is perhaps immediately apparent from the symbolic echoes of real life supervisory activity, the roles of the supervisor and the needs of the supervisee and patient may be quite different in the different domains. Tasks and goals may be quite different depending on what is required. In danger, boundaries may be abrogated in an emergency (e.g. an epileptic fit); in the deficit stage it would depend on what actually needed to be learnt – to keep boundaries or to become more flexible about them (e.g. never ever to change appointment times or to respond to a considered and realistic request).

Of course there are always exceptions.

Conclusion

When we think about the supervisory relationship as a system, this prioritising framework suggests that any supervisory issue can be characterised as primarily concerned with at least one or more of five foci. These are macro sorting capacities, of course, and may overlap, supersede or blend in with one another or others. Furthermore, identifying the type of issue in terms of content or dynamics may be a primary prerequisite to help the supervisee clarify or discover which of these are the most compelling or the most avoided aspects of the supervision.

However, necessary qualifications apart, the suggested framework can provide a useful way of thinking about the supervisory moment in such as way as to enable the supervisee and the supervisor jointly to explore, contract and evaluate interpretations, strategies and possibilities of relationship. The categories can then represent a sequence which can maximise effectiveness in selecting among the myriad of possibilities available to the supervisor.

This is only a map. In the training and supervision of supervisors, this imaginary exercise of course does not obviate the difficulties of choice, decision-making and responsibility. But it can perhaps expand the range and nature of the imaginary and effective realm of the supervisory venture.

References

Airhihenbuwa, C.O., DiClemente, R.J., Wingood, G.M. and Lowe, A. (1992) HIV/AIDS education and prevention among African-Americans: a focus on culture. *AIDS Education and Prevention* 4: 267–76.

Boadella, D. (1988) in *Innovative Therapy in Britain* (eds. J. Rowan and W. Dryden). Buckingham: Open University Press.

Carr, J. (1995) A model of clinical supervision. In *Jungian Perspectives on Clinical Supervision* (ed. P. Kugler) pp. 233–9. Einsiedeln, Switzerland: Daimon.

Clarkson, P. (1975) Seven-level model. Invitational paper delivered at the University of Pretoria, November.

Clarkson, P. (1990) A multiplicity of psychotherapeutic relationships. *British Journal of Psychotherapy* 7(2): 148–63.

Clarkson, P. (1992) *Transactional Analysis Psychotherapy: An Integrated Approach.* London: Routledge.

Clarkson, P. (1993) Two thousand five hundred years of Gestalt – from Heraclitus to the Big Bang, *British Gestalt Journal* 2(1): 4–9.

Clarkson, P. (1994) *The Achilles Syndrome: The Secret Fear of Failure.* Shaftesbury: Element.

Clarkson, P. (1995) *The Therapeutic Relationship in Psychoanalysis, Counselling Psychology and Psychotherapy.* London: Whurr.

Clarkson, P. (1996) *The Bystander (An End to Innocence in Human Relationships?).* London: Whurr.

Clarkson, P. (1997a) Conditions for excellence – the *coincidentia oppositorum* of the inferior function, in *On the Sublime (in Psyche's World)* (ed. P. Clarkson), pp. 219–43. London: Whurr.

Clarkson, P. (1997b) The archetypal situatedness of supervision: parallel process in place. In *On the Sublime (in Psyche's World)* (ed. P. Clarkson), pp. 279–88. London: Whurr.

Clarkson, P. (1997c) Supervision in counselling, psychotherapy and health: an intervention priority sequencing model. *European Journal for Counselling, Psychotherapy and Health*, 1.

Clarkson, P. and Aviram, O. (1997) Phenomenological research in supervision: supervisors reflect on being a supervisor. In *Counselling Psychology: Integrating Theory, Research and Supervised Practice* (ed. P. Clarkson). London: Routledge.

Clarkson, P. and Kellner, K. (1995) Danger, confusion, conflict, and deficit: a framework for prioritising organisational interventions. *Organisations and People* 2(4): 6–13.

Doherty, W.J. (1991) Family therapy goes postmodern. *Family Therapy Networker* 15(5), 37–42.

Ellis, M.V. and Ladany, N. (1997) Inferences concerning supervisees and clients in clinical supervision: an integrative review. In *Handbook of Psychotherapy Supervision* (ed. C.E. Watkins, Jr). New York: Wiley.

Farrell, B.A. (1979) Work in small groups: some philosophical considerations, in *Training in Small Groups: A Study of Five Groups* (eds B. Babington Smith and B.A. Farrell), pp. 103–15. Oxford: Pergamon.

Freud, S. (1960) The psychopathology of everyday life. *Standard Edition* 6. London: Hogarth Press and Institute of Psycho-Analysis.

Helman, C. (1994) *Culture, Health and Illness*, 3rd edn. Oxford: Butterworth-Heinemann.

Kohut, H. (1977) *The Restoration of the Self*. New York: International Universities Press.

McNamee, S. and Gergen, K.J. (1992) *Therapy as Social Construction*. London: Sage.

Robinson, W.L. (1974) Conscious competency – the mark of a competent instructor. *Personnel Journal* 53: 538–9.

Ryle, G. (1966) *Dilemmas: The Tarner Lectures*. Cambridge: Cambridge University Press.

Safran, J.D. (1993) The therapeutic alliance rupture as a transtheoretical phenomenon: definitional and conceptual issues. *Journal of Psychotherapy Integration* 3(1): 33–49.

Searles, H.F. (1955) The informational value of the supervisor's emotional experiences. *Psychiatry* 18: 135–46. (Also in H.F. Searles, *Collected Papers on Schizophrenia and Related Subects*, London: Karnac, 1986.)

Skevington, S.M., MacArthur, P. and Somerset, M. (1997) Developing items for the WHOQOL: an investigation of contemporary beliefs about quality of life related to health in Britain. *British Journal of Health Psychology* 2: 55–72.

Stewart, I. (1996) Signing off. *Tate Magazine* Winter: 80.

Thompson, A. (1990) *Guide to Ethical Practice in Psychotherapy*. Chapter 12. New York: Wiley.

Watkins, C.E. Jr (1997) *Handbook of Psychotherapy Supervision*. New York: Wiley.

Chapter 10
Supervised supervision: including the archetopoi of supervision

PETRŪSKA CLARKSON

Generally it is now considered that specific educational processes or training programmes are necessary for the development of effective supervisors, in addition to their own experience of being supervised. Reviews of the supervision literature and research also support Russell and Petrie's (1994) findings that merely having experience of being a supervisor does not translate into better quality or more competent supervision.

There seems thus to be a specific need in our professions not only for the formation of supervisors but also for the supervision of supervision. Whether such supervision of supervision is envisaged as merely a component of the training programme and/or considered part of one's ongoing professional development will depend on factors in the future too numerous to consider here. I personally do not see supervision of supervision as requiring an endlessly escalating developmental hierarchy. The supervisor may discuss their work with one senior colleague, or with differently specialised consultants at different times, or with a group of peers as consultants. Supervision is the space needed for reflecting on reflection. In my own experience it is the active involvement of colleagues in one's ongoing professional life, a drawing on resources and perspectives outside one's own world view, as well as the opportunity to contribute such vision, support and challenge to others.

In this chapter the work of supervised supervision with a pluralistic orientation is touched on. This is done by means of exploring one theoretical model of supervision - the parallel process - which encapsulates in broad synchronistic terms the transference-countertransference dynamic reflecting across the different subsystems of the supervisory process. It also includes a broader notion still: the idea that the archetypes of place can sometimes carry with them a parallel process offering other ways of integrating or separating or holding simultaneously different psychoanalytic and Jungian theoretical foci.

The interactional field

It is well known that psychotherapists often behave in supervision in the same way the patient behaves in psychotherapy, and that core dynamics of the patient/analyst issues are replicated in some way in the supervisory relationship. Thus, if a patient experiences a sense of helplessness and metaphorically 'leans' on the psychotherapist, the therapist may feel the same helplessness as he or she leans on the supervisor, thus acting out in supervision a transient identification with the patient. This kind of dynamic replication is called parallel process – one of the most influential notions in psychodynamic supervision (Ekstein and Wallerstein, 1972).

Doehrman (1976) investigated this parallel process by conducting clinical interviews of patients, psychotherapists, and supervisors over a period of time. She concluded that the usual understanding goes only half the way. She found that the supervisor stirs the psychotherapist, who then acts out with his or her patients. Thus, parallel process is not reflective alone – it works in both directions. This discovery has just begun to find its way into supervisors' work. It speaks to the complexity of the patient-psychotherapist-supervisor interactions and encourages a humbleness in supervisors. *I* have found that the transference-countertransference dynamic can often seem to encode the parallel process.

A theoretical map (Clarkson, 1992, 1993a; and see Table 10.1) discriminates between:

- what the patient brings to the relationship (proactive transference)
- what the psychotherapist brings (proactive countertransference or therapist transference – pathological)
- what the psychotherapist reacts to in the patient (reactive countertransference – inductive)
- what the patient reacts to as a result of what the psychotherapist brings (patient-countertransference or reactive transference).

As discussed elsewhere (Clarkson, 1993a, 1995), any of these may form the basis for facilitative or destructive psychotherapeutic outcomes. Therefore, because the meaning of a transaction lies in the communicative space *between* the dialoguing partners, it is postulated that a circular interaction serves as the dynamic field for what is called parallel process.

Langs (1976) and Casement (1985) have also shown how, particularly with regard to reactive patient countertransference, patients may be responding to therapists' own induced material. In the same way, supervisees may be part of a projective identification process initiated by supervisors, outside the conscious awareness of either. Hypnotherapists are very familiar with such phenomena and, as Conway and Clarkson (1987) discussed, there are many situations where hypnotic inductions occur in everyday life. Who is hypnotising whom or identifying with whose projection becomes a riddle. What is clear is that this complex interactional process occurs in what Langs (1976) called the *bipersonal field*. But how does this happen when unidirectional causality is challenged?

Jung's notion of synchronicity contributes a particularly valuable way of contextualising this frequently encountered parallel process phenomenon in supervision. It will be remembered that *synchronicity* was defined as an *acausal connecting principle*, 'a "meaningful coincidence" of outer and inner events that are not themselves causally connected' (1964, p. 211). Figure 10.1 attempts to diagrammatise it in a preliminary way.

Parallel process is therefore conceptualised here as a way to describe the pattern of the patient/psychotherapist transference/countertransference relationship or the interpersonal pattern of the dyadic therapeutic relationship as it synchronistically replicates the core dynamics of the client/therapist relationship which is physically absent but psychically present in the supervisory relationship. It happens not only between the client/therapist and the therapist/supervisor pairs, but also between the supervisor or consultant/supervisor pair. The same process tends, in my experience, also to manifest in very similar ways when more people are involved, i.e. in the group dynamic and interplay of transference and countertransference.

Thus the categories and types previously discussed (Clarkson, 1993a) can be seen as the raw material for identifying parallel processes in terms of the interdependent field between patient and psychotherapist. Each category makes either the patient or the therapist the focus of attention in order to facilitate exploration, understanding and intervention design at a particular moment in the therapeutic/supervisory process. However, it must be clear that such division is intrinsically arbitrary and never 'correct' or 'provable'. Patient and therapist processes often interact out of awareness (unconsciously) in ways which may be mutually or differentially influencing each other 'hypnotically' or otherwise. Supervision can be said to exist in order to reflect and learn from this process for the sake of the patient and the professional benefit of the supervisee. So does supervision of supervision.

Specifically, parallel process is the interactional field of the therapist/patient field replicated in the therapist/supervisor field. Any combination of patient and therapist reactions to each other thus forms a dynamic field which is manifested in the supervisory relationship and variously referred to as parallel process (see Figure 10.2).

It is useful to understand the shape and nature of the parallel process

Table 10.1 Examples of transference/countertransference phenomena

Client transference		Proactive type
Complementary (seeks completion)	→ ↘	Client projects actual or fantasised parent or caretaker's past Client projects actual or fantasised past childhood experiences, feelings or fantasies
Concordant (seeks identification)	→	Client projects client's past experience, feelings and fantasies
Destructive	↓	Client's acted out or fantasised destructive past
Facilitative	↑	Client's temperament, liking, style based on past experience

Psychotherapist countertransference		Reactive type
Complementary (seeks completion)	→ ↘	Psychotherapist complements client's real or fantasised projection as caretaker or the childhood experience, feelings or fantasies of client's parent
Concordant (seeks identification)	→	Psychotherapist experiences client's avoided experience or resonates empathically with client's experience
Destructive	↓	Psychotherapist accepts projected identification in destructive way
Facilitative	↑	Psychotherapist's response to client's style or preferences

Psychotherapist (counter)transference		Proactive type
Complementary (seeks completion)	→ ↘	Psychotherapist complements client's real or fantasised projection as caretaker or parent or historical experience based on his/her own past of projects actual or fantasised past experience of caretakers and children
Concordant (seeks identification)	→ ↘	Psychotherapist experiences client's experience based on his/her own past
Destructive	↓	Psychotherapist's past enacted in psychotherapy (therapist's transference) in destructive ways
Facilitative	↑	Psychotherapist's style and personal preferences

Client countertransference		Reactive type
Complementary (seeks completion)	→ ↘	Client completes psychotherapist's real or fantasised projection as caretaker or parent or as child (historical experiences, feeling and fantasies) based on the psychotherapist's past
Concordant (seeks identification)	→	Client experiences psychotherapist's denied child or resonates empathically with therapist's experience
Destructive	↓	Client answers psychotherapist's induced pathology
Facilitative	↑	Client's responses to psychotherapist's preferences and style

This table is an amended and updated version of the summary diagram which was originally published on p. 161 of Clarkson (1992)

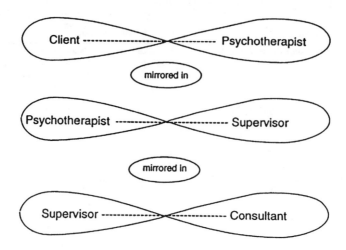

Figure 10.1 Parallel process

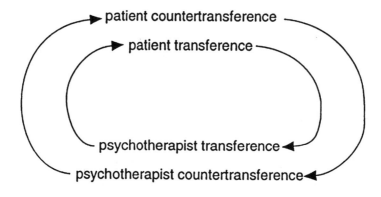

Figure 10.2 The interactional field in context

when it gets in the way of supervision or consulting to supervisors, and to use this knowledge in the prevention of difficulties and the enhancement of learning and effectiveness.

It seemed more accurately representative of the complexity of the patient/therapist field to represent the different forces in it in a circular dynamic relationship to one another. For example, the mutually interacting vectors of transference and countertransference can be illustrated as in Figure 10.2. As we know from physics, the idea that the observer can remain neutral and not influence the observational field is quite disproved (Zohar, 1990). Similarly, it seems obvious that we cannot unequivocally lay the responsibility on the patient for trans-

ferring 'on to or in to the psychotherapist', as if that particular transference could happen with any therapist. Equally it appears clinically
correct that, for many therapists, patients present problems as if they
are acutely aware of the vulnerable areas or developmental tasks of the
therapist, and sometimes they even appear to work in some strange
kind of tandem. Often, as the trainee becomes more in touch with
their negative transference in therapy, for example, so the trainee's
patients become more willing to express anger and disappointment to
the trainee.

To seek definite first causes in such a complex, dynamically interactive situation seems short-sighted. It is more fruitful to recognize
the co-occurrence of such phenomena and their prevalence in many
clinical teaching or supervisory situations. It is interesting to consider
the possibility that a psychotherapist draws to himself or herself the
kind of patients who are most useful for the psychotherapist's development. There is growing and disturbing evidence from modern
physics that unidirectional causality is a highly dubious notion in
explaining physical (or psychological) events. In fact, it seems
increasingly possible that everything is connected with everything
else (Clarkson, 1993b). Jung's (1960) concept of synchronicity
enables our models to serve our ends instead of forcing supervisory
experiences to fit our perceptual prejudices or existing cognitive categories. Herbert (1985) cites the work of John Bell, a theoretical physi-
cist, as follows:

> Despite physicists' traditional rejection of non-local interactions, . . . Bell
> maintains that the world is filled with innumerable non-local influences.
> Furthermore these unmediated connections are present not only in rare and
> exotic circumstances, but underlie all the events of everyday life. Non-local
> connections are ubiquitous because reality itself is non-local. (pp. 214–15).

Because most of these processes are also at the same time unconscious (or out of awareness) and extremely complex, it may be useful
to think about the parallel process as being a *fractal* of the field, that
is, as representing (even though in minute form) the structure of the
larger whole (Gleick, 1988). No matter how small (or large) the size
to which it is reduced (or enlarged), the essential features of the field
will remain present and available for inspection. It is self-similar
across scale. And self-similar across situation. Following these analo-
gies of fractals, or even holons, it is more possible to subject the
dynamic interactional transference/countertransference field to
investigation and use it fruitfully in our work. However, it is important to avoid assigning first causes to either patient or therapist or
supervisor as if these are 'real'.

As the field of supervision grows and develops it also becomes clear that there is only so much one can pay attention to in any given period of time.

The supervision literature offers a multitude of frameworks and theories. The grounds for our choices are often less conscious and less clear than one would wish – particularly in teaching or training supervisors. Of course, no choice is perfect or complete and the supervisee/patient/organisational situation can also change very rapidly. Following from the Intervention Priority Sequencing Model in Chapter 9, the notion developed here is the use of an archetypal image of place or locus to guide and inform our supervision work in terms of some parallel process metaphors.

Within paradigms based on transference-countertransference, it is of course primarily these aspects which provide the information as well as the matrix for the alleviation of the pain or dysfunction, and for learning or development. In my experience it has been most useful to acknowledge the never-ending complexity in theory while in practice focusing on that part of the transference-countertransference dynamic which is most accessible to insight or intervention in the psychotherapy supervision.

Research into whether and how changes made in the supervisory session cause changes back in the consulting room is bedevilled by Doehrman's (1976) finding that the supervisory parallel process dynamic is reflected back into the therapy session as often as not the other way. Furthermore there are numerous anecdotes from experienced supervisors (and supervisees) that apparently inexplicable changes sometimes occur in the psychotheraphy before the psychotherapist has had need or opportunity to implement some interpretation or management plan discussed in the supervision. This is when the supervisee reports a version of 'Patient K must have been listening in to our supervision, because right at the beginning of our next session, he spontaneously referred to the fact that he had suddenly realised/was able to talk about/could remember the dream...'

Casey (1991) has stressed imaginal locality and the spirit of place or 'archetopology' (p. 291). I believe this notion of site or archetypal situatedness can also be fruitfully employed in our clinical work to enliven and enrich the five focal issue categories mentioned in Chapter 9. It may be possible, just for the sake of exploration, to imagine that the work of supervision may also take place in and around different archetypal sites or locations and that particular kinds of parallel process issues have an archetypal locale.

Archytas (in Casey, 1991) wrote that 'Since what is moved is moved into a certain place and doing and suffering are motions it is plain that place, in which what is done and suffered exists, is the first of things' (p. 293). In this way the supervisor/supervisee task, outcome and potential, may depend on the nature of the imaginal space in which the time is spent. It may even be that supervisory sessions which appear to 'go nowhere' or 'get stuck' are those which have 'got lost', wrenched from the appropriate and enhancing spirits of the symbolic place wherein which the supervision could most effectively have taken place. They may not know 'where to go'. This is only a suggestion of a map. In the training and supervision of supervisors, this imaginary exercise does not of course obviate the difficulties of choice, decision-making and responsibility. But it can perhaps expand the range and nature of the imaginary and effective realm of the supervisory venture.

If we pursue this possibility for a brief while, we can use place as a metaphor for the intervention categories of the previous chapter:

- **danger**, the notion of the survival, communication and alliance issues of the tribal hunting grounds
- **confusion**, the idea of the tensions and ambivalence of love and hate in the home or intimate community
- **conflict**, the imagination of the arena – place for combat and tests of strength and cunning
- **deficit**, the leisurely discussions, lively arguments and Socratic dialogues of the olive groves of Academe
- **development**, the sacred precincts of the temple, the hermit's cave, the silence of the inner sanctum of the building or the inner sanctum of the soul.

As Binder and Strupp (1997) write: 'Currently, there is no widespread consensus on the best philosophy and methods for conducting psycho-dynamic supervision. The most prevalent model, however, is characterized by a particular form of integration of didactic and therapeutic roles' (p. 45). Gee (in Chapter 2) has advocated an integration of Kleinian, Freudian and Jungian perspectives, and Samuels (1989) has also articulated a pluralistic vision where different worlds can co-exist in peace and richness. In this small book we have already seen a wide range of supervisors' consultants emphasising, with or without words, different 'spirits of place', each with respective archetypes in attendance at different times and for different purposes.

At any one moment of time, any supervisor may need to be a Cerberus guarding the territories and boundaries, or a Psyche-sorter of the wheat and barley of primary and secondary realities, or a Zeus-like referee between warring internal or external factions, or a Chironic mentor teaching and modelling the skills of healing, or even a Hestian flame of spiritual (professional?) direction. We cannot be all things to all people all of the time. And of course, what is the suitable or right place for one kind of work is not always appropriate – or even safe – for another type. How do we know where to go or where the right arche-

Table 10.2 Summary table – the archetopoi of supervision

Nature of the problem	Locale	Type of focal issue in the parallel process	Role	Primary tasks	Theoretical focus – e.g.	Example
Danger	Hunting grounds	Survival	Cerberus – guardian	Minimise/ obviate danger Manage	Boundaries	The supervisee reports that her depressed client has threatened to kill her child
Confusion	Home/community	Transference Countertransference	Psyche – sorter	Analyse Separate Clarify	Oedipus complex	The client is in an erotic transference with the supervisee
Conflict	Arena	Ambivalence Splitting	Zeus – mediator or referee	Resolve Surrender Integrate Reject or accept	Paranoid-schizoid to depressive position	The patient wishes to terminate analysis. The supervisee vacillates between feeling regretful or relieved at the prospect
Deficit	Academy	Lack (of information, resources, technique, experiences, skill)	Chiron – educator	Enable or intentionally supply information, resources, techniques, access.	Corrective, reparative or developmentally needed experience	The supervisee is worried because they 'broke the boundaries' by accompanying to the police station the patient who had been raped on the way to the session
Development	Temple	Avoidance or exploitation – of mystery *Coincidentia oppositorum*	Hekate exploitation Nature/God/Physis	Allow space for, create a *temenos* or *vas*, enable, acknowledge, the transpersonal dimension (not make archetypal what is, individual or individual what is archetypal)	Collective Unconscious/ archetypal	As a young girl the patient had been ostracised by her fundamentalist religious community for appearing to have caused the death of a younger sibling. She believes she has the devil inside her and that only God can give her absolution

typal place would be for a particular issue? Of course we cannot know for certain. However, we may pay attention to images, associations, dream personifications, symbols, active imagination-involving, counter-transferential fantasies, physical feelings, fears and/or the general atmosphere or *anima loci* which the supervisory session itself evokes as an archetypal resonance – for example, bread, bed, battles, bachelor degrees or cathedral bells.

Thinking, intuition, feeling and sensation naturally all have their parts to play in locating our endeavours most auspiciously. And whether or when we select these foci in terms of the mysterious underworld or the blindingly obvious, always matters of skill, experience and the deep-felt scars and medals of our personal journeys will dictate.

Table 10.2 shows five different kinds of parallel process issues in these terms. According to the archetypal implications of the situatedness for each of these places or locales there is a corresponding theme which in a symbolic way echoes the nature of the problem presented for supervision. Each of these has a corresponding type of focal issue in a parallel process. As a result the supervisor may take different roles depending on the nature of the problem, the *archetopoi* and the parallel process focal issue. The primary tasks and/or theoretical focus will correspondingly differ somewhat – although of course they may always overlap and interlink. For each location I indicate most briefly an example of a corresponding kind of presentation by the supervisee of a client issue which could emerge in supervised supervision. This table is simply indicative; it may, however, suggest comparisons or alternatives to other supervisors.

Naturally, supervisory exploration in depth may make it clear that a problem does not belong in its original place of presentation but in another archetypal locale. Supervised supervision is a vast subject, and so is the development of any Jungian archetypal approach to supervision. The examples shown here are simply for the purposes of initial demonstration and to start a conversation, not to close it.

References

Binder, J.L. and Strupp, H.H. (1997) Supervision of Psychodynamic Psychotherapies, in C.E. Watkins, Jr. (ed.) *Handbook of Psychotherapy Supervision*, pp. 44–62, New York, Wiley.

Casement, P. (1985) *On Learning from the Patient*. London: Tavistock.

Casey, E.S. (1991) *Spirit and Soul: Essays in Philosophical Psychology*. Dallas, TX: Spring Publications.

Clarkson, P. (1992) *Transactional Analysis Psychotherapy: An Integrated Approach*. London: Routledge.

Clarkson, P. (1993a) Through the looking glass: explorations in transference and countertransference. In *On Psychotherapy*, pp. 177–90, London: Whurr.

Clarkson, P. (1993b) New perspectives in counselling and psychotherapy (or adrift in a sea of change), in *On Psychotherapy*, pp. 209–232. London: Whurr.

Clarkson, P. (1995) The transference/countertransference relationship, in *The Therapeutic Relationship*, pp. 62–107, London: Whurr.

Conway, A. and Clarkson, P. (1987) Everyday hypnotic inductions. *Transactional Analysis Journal* 17(2), 17-23.

Doehrman, M.J. (1976) Parallel processess in supervision and psychotherapy. *Bulletin of the Menninger Clinic*, 40, 9–104.

Ekstein, R. and Wallerstein, R.S. (1972) *The Teaching and Learning of Psychotherapy* (2nd edn.). Madison, CT: International Universities Press.

Gleick, J. (1988) *Chaos: Making a New Science*. London: Heinemann.

Herbert, N. (1985) *Quantum Reality: Beyond the New Physics*. London: Anchor Press/Doubleday.

Hess, A.K. (ed.) (1980) *Psychotherapy Supervision: Theory, Research and Practice*. New York: John Wiley.

Jung, C.G. (1960) Synchronicity: An acausal connecting principle. *Collected Works* 8, pp. 417–531, London: Routledge and Kegan Paul.

Jung, C.G. (1964) *Man and His Symbols*. London: Aldus.

Langs, R. (1976) *The Bipersonal Field*. New York: Jason Aronson.

Russell, R.K. and Petrie, T. (1994) Issues in training effective supervisors. *Applied and Preventive Psychology* 3, 27–42.

Samuels, A. (1989) *The Plural Psyche*. London: Routledge.

Zohar, D. (1990) *The Quantum Self*. London: Bloomsbury.

Index